The
LABRADOR RETRIEVER

Edited by
DAVID CRAIG

BEST of BREED

ACKNOWLEDGEMENTS

The publisher would like to thank the following for help with photography: Ann Britton (Bowstones), David Coode (Warringah), Fiona Hillman (Penworlod), Erica Jayes (Sandylands), Jo Williams (Kativa), Canine Partners for Independence, Defence Animal Centre, Dogs for the Disabled, Pets as Therapy, Support Dogs, and David Tomlinson for his excellent photos of working Labradors.
page 49 © istockphoto.com/Waldemar Dabrowski
page 63 © istockphoto.com/Waldemar Dabrowski
page 90 © istockphoto.com/Leigh Schindler
page 92 © istockphoto.com/Waldemar Dabrowski
page 102 © istockphoto.com/Hedda Gjerpen

Cover photo: © Tracy Morgan Animal Photography (www.animalphotographer.co.uk)

The British Breed Standard reproduced in Chapter 7 is the copyright of the Kennel Club and published with the club's kind permission. Extracts from the American Breed Standard are reproduced by kind permission of the American Kennel Club.

THE QUESTION OF GENDER
The 'he' pronoun is used throughout this book in favour of the rather impersonal 'it', but no gender bias is intended.

First published in 2008 by The Pet Book Publishing Company Limited
PO Box 8 Lydney Gloucestershire GL15 6YD

Reprinted 2009 and 2010 with amendments.
This edition published 2011

ISBN
978-1-906305-21-5
1-906305-21-8

Printed and bound in China through Printworks Int. Ltd.

CONTENTS

GETTING TO KNOW LABRADOR RETRIEVERS

Chapter 1

Imagine you had arrived from another planet, had never heard of a Labrador Retriever, and had picked up this book by accident. My remit is to "introduce the Labrador", so here goes…

While mentioning other planets – the nearest I have come to another planet was spending a few days in Tokyo prior to judging Labradors. Despite the world-famous Japanese hospitality and kindness, I was feeling quite homesick. Anyone who has been lucky enough to visit Japan will know what I mean about a culture shock. While I had the most wonderful time, the most precious memory of that trip was the very

What makes a Labrador so special?

THE RETRIEVER BREEDS

Labrador Retriever

Golden Retriever

emotional feeling I got when the first class of Labradors came into the ring to be judged and I saw the familiar happy expressions, the wagging tails, and the typical temperament. At that moment I knew that nothing else in the world could have made me so welcome and at home as this wonderful breed. Once more I marvelled at the Labrador's adaptability – there's not much space in Tokyo for a gundog!

To even try to introduce the Labrador seems a bit of a con, as most people the world over know exactly what they *imagine* a Labrador looks like and how he behaves. Labradors, more than almost any other breed, are all things to all people, and to some degree there are almost breeds within the breed.

Ask the man in the street the questions "What are Labradors?" and "What can Labradors do?"

and he may mention "the Andrex puppy", that Labradors "like children", that they are "shooting dogs" or, more likely, "guiding dogs". Often, there would be a reference to kindness, good temperament or trainability.

Let's consider what makes the Labrador my breed of choice, or even perhaps the right breed for you. Firstly, I think we should consider what he isn't. Well, he isn't a guard dog. That said, in 30 years of living with seven or eight of them at a time, there have been two occasions that have shown me that, when the chips are down, they will even give that job their best shot. The other thing a Lab isn't, quite obviously, is a pocket or handbag dog, as is the current fad of young celebrities – so at least his size has saved him from that! He isn't really a lap dog, although all of our Labs are regularly lifted up

on to laps by the male members of the family to lie horizontal, feet sticking out, to get their tummies rubbed. But perhaps the biggest misconception is that the Labrador arrives on this earth fully trained, peaceful and a model citizen. That brings us to the end of the short list of what he isn't!

SO WHAT IS A LABRADOR?

To help us understand the breed, and then to look at type, it may help to examine how breeds are classified. This is a system operated by national kennel clubs, and there may be slight differences in classification depending on where you live.

Breeds are divided into seven groups roughly equating to their purpose/use, and then into sub-groups. The Labrador Retriever forms part of the Gundog Group

Chesapeake Bay Retriever   **Flat Coated Retriever**   **Curly Coated Retriever**

(known as the Sporting Group in the US), and within this group it comes in the sub-group of Retrievers. His title and classification tell us a great deal about how the breed was originally developed. He is a gundog, specialising in retrieving game. While describing the Gundog Group, it is worth considering his closest relations within the Retriever sub-group. They are: the Flat Coated Retriever (black and liver), the Golden Retriever (golden) and his rarer cousins the Curly Coated Retriever (black and liver) and the Chesapeake Bay (any shade of brown). It is interesting to note that they are all very similar in size and shape and were often interbred. The colours are also interesting genetically, as they are in the same group of alleles, showing that you don't need to dig too far

to find the links between the various breeds of retriever.

I find it fascinating, when looking at Labs, to spot the various traits, particularly the traits we see as 'foreign' but, in fact, tell us much about the dogs' ancestry. It's not that unusual to see a Flat Coat head or a wavy or curly coat in the breed even today. You therefore don't have to try too hard to see that all of the retriever breeds, not too many generations ago, were interbred. The puppies most resembling one breed becoming that breed, yet having brothers or sisters recognised as another breed. Of course, this couldn't happen today in Kennel Club registered dogs. Unlike many breeds, the Labrador as a registered breed is not particularly old. It was first recognised by the Kennel Club (UK) just over 100 years ago. But once established, it quickly grew

in numbers, and has remained at the top of pedigree registrations in the UK and in North America for the last 10 years.

The breed the Labrador is most commonly confused with is its cousin, the Golden Retriever. This, I believe, is for two reasons: firstly the name and secondly the colour. Many people refer to yellow Labradors as 'golden Labradors'; plus they both have the word 'retriever' in their name. When a potential puppy buyer asks for a "Golden Labrador Retriever" it is often worth checking if they want a long-coated or a short-coated one! This usually clears up the confusion; those looking for long-coated dogs are sent to Golden Retriever breeders, while those looking for short-coated dogs are taught the correct description. It sounds pedantic, but it does avoid confusion.

Black: The original
Labrador colour.

LABRADOR COLOURS

Yellow: This may range from light
cream to red fox.

Chocolate: This colour is becoming
increasingly popular

Physically, the Labrador is a medium/large-sized short-coated dog, coming in three whole colours: black, yellow or chocolate. Depending on whether he is bred as a working dog or as a show dog, he weighs in at anything between 25-40 kg (55-88 lb) with the majority of quality dogs coming in at around 30-35 kg (66-77 lb). The average height measurement is 53-56 cm at the shoulder (21-22 inches). A Labrador, quite simply, is a dog-shaped dog, free from exaggeration and excess. He's not too big or too small, with a shortish coat, meaning he doesn't bring too much of the outdoors, indoors with him. So, really, his looks are nothing special.

Even the preceding paragraph could provoke a debate. While thinking how to approach this chapter, I found a vet who claims that her Labrador dog in good condition for Crufts weighed 19 kg! I find it impossible to imagine a dog weighing 19 kg (42 lb) in good condition conforming to the Breed Standard. I also found kennels in America that are selling eight different colours of Labradors. This just goes to show that nothing is as straightforward as it looks!

LABRADOR HOMES
In the UK, 45,000-plus Labradors are registered with the Kennel Club every year; in the USA the current registration figures stand at nearly 124,000. So where do all these dogs end up?

THE PET HOME
The vast majority, perhaps as many as 90 per cent of the Labradors registered each year, find their way into pet homes. It behoves all breeders to keep this in mind when deciding a dog's suitability for breeding and matching it with a breeding partner.

The vast majority of Labradors bred every year go to pet homes.

A WORKING GUNDOG HOME

This type of home probably accounts for around five or six per cent of the pups born each year. I am delighted to say that many Labs still fulfil the role the breed was developed for: that of a working gundog. Indeed, I would go so far as to claim that they are the most popular of the working gundog breeds. Be it picking-up, rough shooting, wildfowling or even beating, a Labrador is often first choice.

Within this group, I feel there must be a sub-division for field trial dogs. While genuine gundog work has changed very little over the last 100 years, modern field trials have become specialised areas and should be considered as a separate sport.

A SHOW HOME

This accounts for probably three to five per cent per year. Show dogs need to meet the criteria laid down in the Breed Standard in every way, and competition is tough.

SPECIALISED WORKING HOMES

Probably around one or two per cent per year in this group. I have included dogs for the disabled, sniffer dogs (i.e. the various detection dogs) and, of course, guide dogs.

TOP DOG

What are the qualities that make the Labrador the most popular dog in the world? A Labrador who has had time spent on him will list among his attributes: his will to please; his useful nose, which can be trained to scent anything from game to mobile phones; his gentle gaze when all is not well in your world; his love of a game of football with the kids; and the ease with which he accepts new arrivals, be they adults, children or other pets. These are the qualities that make him stand out from the crowd and put him high on the list for families wanting a pet, anyone who wants to go game shooting, and, of course, those needing support dogs.

Couple all of these virtues with the fact that the Labrador is fairly low-maintenance. Although he is quite a big dog, his exercise requirements in a pet home are pretty undemanding, even by modern lifestyle standards. A brisk walk of 20 to 30 minutes, mixed with some time off-lead morning and night, will suffice as long as the dog has access to a garden or yard a couple of other times during the day. At the weekend, a longer walk will be appreciated and will help to keep a Labrador in good condition. The Labrador is also undemanding in terms of grooming, in so much as the coat doesn't mat and doesn't need trimming. However, when a Labrador is casting his coat, which usually occurs twice a year, you will certainly know about it. The best way to counter the problem is to brush your Labrador on a daily basis at this time.

The Labrador fulfilling its original role as a working gundog.

THE RIGHT CHOICE

Before you rush out and buy a Labrador, don't make the mistake of thinking that it is a 'one size fits all' breed, or that one Labrador is much the same as another. The Labrador is like a diamond, precious and many faceted, and can be made into whatever you want. But just like a diamond, it helps to know what you want to turn it into before you start. This diversity of type should, maybe, be seen as a good thing, as it means people can have exactly the sort of Labrador they want.

Over the years I have had the pleasure of living with many Labradors, and I have never had two the same. They do have many similar characteristics, which are passed down strains, lines and types. Do some research and find out why the various types have been developed and why the physical

and mental attributes have become linked. If you don't start with an understanding of how the different types have developed, you can't begin to work out what type will suit your lifestyle. This may seem a difficult concept to grasp, but less so when you think about it. For many generations, breeders have been selectively choosing the dogs that most suit their purpose. Strains have been developed by people who want to specialise, and with specialisation inevitably comes change – both in looks, brains and character.

As a rough division, there are the breeders who breed for looks, and the breeders who breed for brains. Of course, this is an overly simplistic view. It must be remembered that a dog can be honed to fit in with an owner's lifestyle and the work he is required to do. In just the same

way, you will need to hone your pup to fit in with your lifestyle. All breeders avoid extremes of temperament because it produces dogs that no one wants.

There are also breeders who like to make their lives even more difficult and breed for both brains and beauty. These dual-purpose breeders try to steer a middle course, avoiding the extremes at both ends but in doing so may be denied the top-winning dog in either sphere.

WORKERS AND LOOKERS

When people make that initial phone call, to see if a breeder has pups to sell, they will often refer to the two basic types, and describe them roughly as: "The big ones with a square head" and "the small, lighter ones". The problems arise when the people looking for the former want to work their dog, and the people looking for the latter want to

The smaller, lighter, working Labrador needs an outlet for his energies.

show. As I have tried to make clear, the potential purchaser who is looking for "a big, heavy one with a square head" and the would-be buyer who is looking for "a smaller, lighter one" are in danger of ignoring the temperament that often goes along with the different types. If the physical attributes are driving the purchaser, they may be unhappy with the accompanying mental qualities.

The smaller, lighter type, due to its working background, is also likely to be the busier, brainier dog and need more mental stimulation and exercise. Field Trial Champions in the first and second generation of a pedigree should be seen as the Ferraris of the breed. I would think carefully about their suitability as pets, particularly for the first-time owner. They have been bred to be energetic and to use their brains; they can be overly sensitive and too highly strung. Brains and energy can be a potent mixture.

The heavier, squarer type, seen in the show ring, may be content with less exercise, and may be more peaceable around the house. By nature, show dogs need to be confident and outgoing and this can be a very good thing in a pet home. However, the temperament required to keep a show dog on his toes, wagging his tail non-stop for the length of a class (which may last over an hour), can lead to some of the dogs being 'showing fools' and a bit giddy. If you are looking for a working gundog, the show type will probably take longer to train, and it may never work with the speed and panache of the working-type Labrador. This shows how important it is to understand the rudiments of 'type', and the way in which it has become linked to purpose, in order to avoid making a fundamental mistake. This does not mean that all trial-bred dogs are overly sensitive, or that all show dogs are hectic, but 'buyer beware'. Temperaments run in families, and if the parents' temperaments are not what you want, the pups are unlikely to be suitable.

One of the mysteries of Labrador breeding is the amount of coat that show dogs carry compared to working-bred dogs. You would expect the breeders of working dogs to have retained the correct weather- and water-proof coat as described in the Breed Standard to protect their dogs. In fact, you are more likely to find short, single coats in the workers than in the show-bred Labrador. Look at the photos showing Buccleuch Avon and Nell (page 26) who both have lots of bone and substance and

The Labradors seen in the show ring tend to be heavier with a squarer head.

BRED FOR THE JOB?

I always find it rather embarrassing in my boarding kennel for the few days after Crufts when my customers ask, "What did you think of the Labrador?" Often, when I say I thought it was very nice, they comment on how fat it was! In defence of the show Labrador, most are not as fat as you would imagine – although, I do not mean to defend them fully. Some are clearly not capable of doing the job they were bred for and are overweight – but these are not usually the winners. Please remember as well, this breed should have a very thick coat and a thick skin, which adds to the picture of solidness. Anyone will tell you that appearing on television adds pounds – although I can't explain why it only happens to Labradors!

very thick coats before deciding whether the show dogs of today are so very different from their ancestors 100 years ago.

The link between type and history is also illustrated by the Labrador's famous appetite. The Labrador's ancestors had to survive harsh winters, living on scraps (see Chapter 2: The First Labrador Retrievers), so we shouldn't be surprised by the fact that the Labrador is the ultimate canine dustbin, with a metabolism that would challenge the most committed anorexic.

Somehow in selecting for solid looks, breeders have fixed the fat gene more in the show lines than the working lines. Labradors are among the best food converters in the canine world, and this must go back to their origins when food would have been in very short supply. The dogs that could convert an odd fish head into a good meal, and survive, would possibly be the only ones still alive to be bred from at the end of the harsh winters in Newfoundland. Therefore, the pet Labrador that is fed on high-

quality foods and lives in a warm, centrally heated home is always in danger of piling on the pounds.

THE IDEAL PET HOME
Pet homes come in all shapes and sizes, and trying to describe the ideal home is like trying to describe the ideal Labrador. A Labrador needs space, but it is not always the biggest house, with the largest garden, that offers the best home. Over the years, I have placed puppies in a variety of homes, but the best

homes have three things in common:

• **The time spent with the dog**
Labradors thrive on human companionship, and a dog that is involved in his owner's life and shares his activities will be a happy Lab.

• **The effort put into keeping the dog mentally and physically healthy**
To keep a Labrador healthy, he must be exercised regularly and kept at the right weight. In addition, the exercise should be adjusted to suit the age of the dog. (One of my pet hates is to see dogs, at either end of their life be they pups or oldies, being trailed around on the end of a lead – you wouldn't do it to a child or your granny, why do it to your dog?) A Labrador also needs mental stimulation, and if you are not involved in a sport, such as obedience or agility, you can stimulate your dog by teaching him party tricks or playing fun games, such as hide-and-seek or retrieve.

• **The sense not to keep a beloved dog going for too long at the end of its life**
This is a hard one, and I can understand people wondering why this is so high on my list of what makes a good home. But I have seen some terrible cruelty in the name of care and kindness. I talk to people who have my dogs about this problem right from the start, because, unfortunately, not all dogs make old age. The caring owner must always put the dog first.

These are the things that make a good home for me, not the physical space available. Indeed, as a garden is no place to exercise a Labrador; it has no place on my list of requirements for ideal homes, be they pet, show or working homes. The most important criterion is spending time with your dog; no Labrador can adapt to solitary confinement. If all you want is a dog to sit at home for eight hours a day while you are out at work, get an ornament instead.

A Labrador loves nothing more than spending time with his people.

CAREER DOGS

Labradors make ideal assistance dogs and can be trained to help with a diverse range of tasks, from collecting the post and the milk, to paying for food at the weekly shop.

CAREER DOGS

The Labrador Retriever's sound, biddable temperament makes him ideal for working closely with people, and the breed is highly valued in a number of working disciplines.

GUIDE DOGS

Guide dog charities throughout the world are united in finding the Labrador Retriever an ideal choice for this demanding work. The Labrador is easy to train and is the perfect size for guiding work.

A Labrador will form a strong bond with his owner, and this is vital in creating good working partnerships. Often, the Labradors are crossed with Golden Retrievers, and this also produces dogs that are well suited to guiding work.

ASSISTANCE DOGS

The Labrador has proved an excellent choice as an assistance dog, working with people who are wheelchair bound or who have other disabilities. The dogs are trained to perform task work, such as picking up dropped items, fetching the post, or helping their owner to get dressed and undressed. They can open doors, push buttons for lifts, and will also 'speak' to sound the alarm in an emergency. Labradors are also being used as assistance dogs with children, and this is proving hugely successful.

HEARING DOGS

A hearing dog is trained to alert his owner to a variety of everyday sounds. These can include:
• The doorbell
• The telephone
• A cooker timer
• A smoke alarm
• A baby monitor.

A hearing dog must be alert to all sounds and have a strong bond with his owner.

The Labrador's sense of smell is put to good use. Here, a Lab is searching for explosives.

The Labrador bonds strongly with his owner and has proved to be very successful in this field.

SNIFFER DOGS

Prisons have found Labradors and English Springer Spaniels, as well as other gundog breeds, useful for what they term 'active drug detection'. The Labrador is often first choice for passive detection work, i.e. in waiting rooms and among civilians, particularly family members with children who may be visiting prisons. As well as great noses necessary for the work, Labradors are generally viewed by the public as being people-friendly and are therefore not found threatening in any way. Sniffer dogs are also widely used in airports and ports, searching for drugs and explosives.

SEIZURE ALERT DOGS

Many breeds and crossbreeds are being tried for this role and, yet again, Labradors have been selected. This area is still undergoing investigation, as it is difficult to know if dogs are 'scenting' changes or picking up on body language.

To me, the best Labrador is a friend, a servant and a willing helper, and the following sums up the very, very best of Labradors. I am delighted that Endal, a truly remarkable Labrador, was named Dog of the Millennium and that his ancestry has been traced back through 26 generations, to the original Buccleuch Labradors (see Chapter 2). What a testament and tribute to the wonderful breeders who have developed this many-faceted breed and given us the truly remarkable dogs we have today – just like Allen Parton, many Labrador owners are better people for having let the breed into their life.

ENDAL
The Dog That Changed My Life
by Allen Parton

I served for 18 years with the Royal Navy as a weapons engineering officer and was reckoned to have good career prospects. I was also happy at home; I was married with two children. But it was while serving in the Royal Navy during the Gulf War in 1991 that I was involved in a road accident. The serious head injury I sustained led me to be in hospital/rehab for the following five years. The sum of my condition was that I couldn't recall getting married or the birth of my children. My memory only lasts four days and I've lost forever 50 per cent of my life history. I am in a wheelchair, I have difficulty reading and writing, and, until I met Endal, I couldn't talk. I didn't have the emotions of love, hate, happiness or sadness. None of the memories lost have returned.

I was in the darkest, most soulless place a person can be without hope. Endal, a year-old yellow Labrador, bounced into that dark place and said to me with his shining eyes, "Hold on to me and I'll drag you out of here", and to this very day he has never stopped dragging. He has taught me to love, laugh and cry again. He brought happiness into my sadness, love where there was none, and a zest for life that has changed me. He does not see the disability; his love is unconditional, and if you could capture the healing power of his love, you would cure the world of all its evils.

If I fall unconscious out of my wheelchair, Endal will put pull me into the recovery position, cover me with a blanket and set off the emergency telephone. If nothing happens, he will then open the window and bark for help to the neighbours. If that does not work, he will open the door and fetch help.

He understands signing, which I have to use because I forget the name of items - i.e. touching my head means hat,

Endal is one of the most skilled assistance dogs, and can even operate a cash machine.

touching my hand means gloves, and rubbing the side of my face means electric razor. If I forget to shut the fridge door, he comes behind me and closes it; if I go to cross a road without looking, he stops me. He can operate the cashpoint machine for me: he puts the card in and takes the card, money and receipt out for me. When we go into the pub, he will take my wallet and jump up to the bar and bark until he is served. He buys the ticket on the bus, and collects the ticket from the machine.

He was not trained to do many of these tasks, but he has responded to my needs. He takes items off the supermarket shelf, puts them in my basket, and, at the checkout, puts them on the belt. He then takes my wallet up to pay for me. He can help undress me. He operates lights, lift buttons and opens and shuts doors. He opens the washing machine, unloads it, and then passes me items to be pegged out.

To date, he has had 64 film crews from around the world, spending a minimum of two days each with him. He has won many titles: Dog of the Millennium, Dog of the Year Winner of the Golden Bonio 2000, and Year of Promise 'life-saver award'.

Endal operates the train door for Allen.

THE FIRST LABRADOR RETRIEVERS

Chapter 2

So you're thinking of buying a Labrador – why a Labrador? Probably because you have heard about their excellent temperament and character, and how they are the ideal family dogs, happy to join in with everything we do. Have you ever wondered why this is? Where a breed originated, and why it became that 'breed' has a direct bearing on the dog we know today. The Labrador looks and behaves like it does simply because of its origins, and how 'we' have developed it over many years.

Wolves had to hunt, chase and kill to stay alive. As years went by and dogs evolved, they were far more likely to live in the company of man. They would still hunt, chase and kill, but also share our food. As breeds developed, we used these instincts to hunt for our benefit. Some of the hound breeds have

an inbuilt instinct to chase and kill, even today. Terriers will hunt and kill vermin. But in our retriever breeds we have selected a dog that will hunt, let us kill, and then they will fetch it to us.

LABRADOR ROOTS

There are many theories as to how the Labrador Retriever came into existence. In spite of its name, the Labrador did not originate from Labrador, but from Newfoundland. This is very much open to debate, as first reports in 1497, when John Cabot 'discovered' Newfoundland, recorded an absence of dogs among the natives. In fact the native Dorset Eskimos had been there some 3,000 years before Newfoundland was discovered by Cabot. There are also reports of the Beothucks, the natives of Newfoundland, having wolf-like dogs. The Beothucks were there when the first Europeans

travelled to Newfoundland, but by the early 1800s these people had virtually disappeared.

The first European discoverers had taken dogs on their ships and these could easily have bred with any local dogs, if there were any, and become ancestors of the later dogs. Some years on, sailors and fishermen from England and parts of Europe (France, Portugal and Spain) began to travel regularly to Newfoundland to fish the highly productive cod banks. The different nationalities settled in their own areas around the Newfoundland coast; there was such an abundance of fish that they need never stray into another area.

Significantly, the English fished close to the shores, while other nationalities were deep-sea fishers. The English fished from small dory boats that were much lower to the water than the large ships. These boats were probably made on land and then stored over each winter to be repaired for the next season. The use of dogs on the smaller boats probably also gives a clue to these animals being of a medium size, as there would not have been very much room on board to accommodate larger dogs. The dogs would need a short, oily, dense coat to keep them warm and dry. The water-resistant coat also prevented too much water coming into the boats when the dogs were hauled back onboard by the scruff of the neck.

The English also worked on the land, in order to dry and cure their catches with salt. They chose an area known as Avalon, on the south-eastern peninsular of Newfoundland; the area they fished was mainly to the east. Powerful merchants employed the fishermen, although to many of those men it was probably more like slavery. They would sail out each spring, returning home with their dry, salted catches later in the year. However, the merchants did not allow any of their men to settle on the land. In fact, the ships' masters were fined for every man who did not return to England on their ships. The reason for this was because the merchants were worried that the fishermen might set up on their own and be in direct competition – though how the fishermen would have

The Labrador's oily, water-resistant coat kept him warm and dry.

built large, commercial ships to sail back to Europe is a mystery.

Every spring a temporary 'government' was formed, and the captain of the first ship to arrive at its destination was given the title of 'fishing admiral' for that season. He was in charge of all the English ships and those people who worked ashore. During each winter, woodworkers and carpenters were left on shore, preparing wharves, and building and

repairing boats and sheds for the fishermen's return the following spring.

At one point, during Charles 1's reign (1625-1649), a law was passed that prohibited anyone from settling within six miles of the coast. This law was enforced by the British navy. Another law made it impossible for anyone to settle permanently by stating that no building could possess a stone chimney. This meant that no fires could be used to heat homes and cook food, so settlers would have found it impossible to survive. The men who were left behind to work over the winters must have lived a very tough life. Over the years, the Newfoundland population did grow, with men and women jumping ship and deserting.

In 1713, the Treaty of Utrecht gave England the sovereignty of Newfoundland. By the end of the 1700s, large groups were declaring their independence and heading inland, where they were safer. Their only laws were their own, and wrongdoers were hanged and flogged. But even as late as 1800, the British navy would still capture deserters and hang them from the yardarm. The native Beothucks did not survive this onslaught by the settlers, who killed them for sport. Yet through all those years, English and European fishing vessels and their crews were sent to Newfoundland to bring back the huge catches from the wonderfully productive waters. And so this was the land and background from which our future Labradors were to emerge.

FISHERMEN'S FRIEND

There was an opposing view, stating that it was over 200 years before any dog was recorded as being seen in Newfoundland. Whether or not this was true, we cannot be sure, but the fishermen found dogs that became of use to them. These dogs were of two types: one was a heavy-built dog with a longer coat, and the second type was lighter and smaller but strongly built and possessed a shorter, very dense

coat. The heavier dog was probably what we now call the Newfoundland, whereas the lighter-built one became known as the St John's Dog in England, the Water Dog in Newfoundland, but was eventually named the Labrador some time after its arrival in England.

It was found that the lighter-built dogs were ideal to help the fishermen with their work. These dogs had no trouble swimming in the freezing waters (their weather-resistant, waterproof coats protected them, and their otter-like tails acted as rudders), where they delivered messages between boats, helped to pull the ropes and nets in the sea, and retrieved fish that escaped from the nets. They were possibly also

used as sledge dogs. This will-to-please was what made them so useful, and that same temperament typifies the breed today. Many breeds that work do so for themselves, but the Labrador does it for us. The dogs from Newfoundland also had to exist on very poor diets. Today, the Labrador is still a compulsive scavenger!

Following its independence from Great Britain in 1783, America was able to fish in the waters off Newfoundland. This resulted in reduced catches for the English, but as the ships sailed back to England in the early 1800s – notably to Poole harbour on the south coast of Britain – they took some of the dogs with them. Although they

The heavier-built dogs with longer coats developed into the breed we know as Newfoundlands.

The first Labradors were thrown from fishing boats and swam ashore.

were mainly black, there were reports of rust-coloured dogs. The noted British sportsman, Colonel Hawker, wrote: "he is oftener black than of other colours". The recessive yellow gene may already have been in the early imported dogs. There is some evidence to show that there may have been a few other colours, such as blacks with markings on them, and brindling. There is every likelihood that yellows existed even then, originating from the Portuguese breed, the Cane di Castro Laboreiro – there is certainly a strong resemblance to the early yellow Labradors.

As a direct result of the Atlantic fishing trade, Poole developed into a major, prosperous port. There is reference to both St John's Dogs and Newfoundlands being used for cart-hauling in Poole, and also a number of them being used to pull the carts as far as London to deliver fish. In about 1850 this was made illegal. It did not take the sea captains long to realise that the dogs they brought back to England could earn them extra money, and the import of dogs became a regular trade. When the sea captains arrived in Poole, they would transfer the dogs to gigs and row ashore. The signal that the dogs were for sale was when the dogs were thrown overboard and started swimming for land.

However, British customs soon realised what was going on and put duty on the dogs. It was therefore less profitable to import dogs, and the trade dwindled.

BREED PIONEERS
It was the 2nd Earl of Malmesbury (1778-1841), who lived at Heron Court, near Poole, who was the first to see the true potential in the imported dogs. He was an outstanding sportsman, and he quickly realised that here was a dog who was capable of retrieving shot and wounded 'game', both on land and from water. By 1809, he was using dogs from Newfoundland as

Cane di Castro Laboreiro: Note the resemblance to early yellow Labradors.

working gundogs. He called them the 'Little Newfoundlanders', but it was apparently his son, the 3rd Earl of Malmesbury, who re-named them 'Labradors'. News of the Labrador's ability spread to the north of England and to Scotland, and other landowners with shooting estates started using them. From working in the south, retrieving duck and geese from water and marshland, the breed progressed to land-work, working on 'game' birds and ground game. But with the limited importation, many of the early dogs were interbred with other retriever types. The original bloodlines were diluted to such an extent that the dogs were simply referred to as Retrievers.

Fortunately, the Malmesbury dogs were bred without crossing them with any other breeds. From these first dogs the breed began as we know it. There is a record around 1835 of some of the early dogs going to the 5th Duke of Buccleuch, in Scotland, and his family have carried the line on through many generations, right up to the present day. The Buccleuch Labradors of recent times trace directly back to the Malmesbury dogs. It seems that the first written mention of the Labrador was in 1839 when the 5th Duke of Buccleuch wrote that he had taken his 'Labrador' Moss to

Heron Court: Home of the 2nd Earl of Malmesbury.

Nell (aged 11), owned by the Earl of Home.

Buccleuch Avon: The Buccleuch bloodlines trace directly to the Malmesbury dogs.

Naples on his yacht, and that the 10th Lord Home took his 'Labrador' Drake as well. In 1867 a photograph was taken of the Earl of Home's 'Nell' (aged about 11 years), who appears to be a very typical Labrador – one we would easily recognise today.

Other well-known breeders at that time were the Hon. Arthur Holland-Hibbert, who became the 3rd Viscount Knutsford, and the famous Mrs Quintin Dick, who later became Lorna, Countess Howe (Banchory). The Hon. Arthur Holland-Hibbert bought his first Labrador bitch, Sybil, in 1884, sired by Sir Fredrick Graham's Kielder. Sybil was then bred to a Malmesbury dog and this founded the famous Munden kennel.

By 1880 the fishing trips to Newfoundland were lessening because people were now emigrating to Newfoundland and starting up their own fishing trade with southern European countries. In 1885 the Newfoundland Sheep Protection Act was brought in to protect the sheep population. This meant that families were only allowed to keep one dog. A higher duty was imposed on bitch pups, and so they were killed at birth, hence the population dropped considerably. In 1895, quarantine laws were passed in Britain, so any dogs coming into the country had to undergo a lengthy six-month confinement. These factors marked the decline in the numbers of dogs being brought to England.

Before the Labrador came to England, the most popular dogs for shooting purposes were Spaniels, Curly Coated Retrievers, and Retrievers. The black and liver-coloured Retrievers were more on the lines of Flat Coated Retrievers, as we know them today. Some early Labradors were crossed with these Retrievers and even Pointers, and possibly several other breeds, but the significant early breeders of the Labrador kept them pure. Indeed in 1887 a letter from the 3rd Earl of Malmesbury to 6th Duke of Buccleuch states: "We always call mine Labrador dogs and I have kept the breed as pure as I could from the first I had from Poole... known by their having a close coat which turns the water off like oil and, above all, a tail like an otter." It is probably due to the third Earl not crossing or interbreeding his Labradors that

Ben of Hyde: The first registered yellow Labrador.

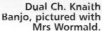

Dual Ch. Knaith Banjo, pictured with Mrs Wormald.

we have the breed we know today. It must have been extremely difficult to keep a kennel such as this pure, with the limited number of dogs available. The mid-1880s was not an easy time for the breed and it may even have come close to dying out.

It is understood that a small number of liver-coloured Labrador puppies were starting to appear in black litters, but they didn't prove popular as working dogs, and, in most cases, they were destroyed. In 1892 there is a record of two liver-coloured pups being born at the Buccleuch kennels. It was noted that even if the Labrador was crossed with another breed, in many cases the resulting pups took after the Labrador side of their pedigree. It is difficult to

prove this, but even today we can see Labradors who have some small features that give away the fact that they may have other bloodlines – such as Flat Coat, Curly Coat, Golden Retriever, or Pointer – some way back in their ancestry.

Occasionally, yellow pups appeared in litters, and, like the liver pups, they were quietly disposed of. It wasn't until 1899 that the first yellow Labrador was registered: Ben of Hyde, bred by Major C.J. Radclyffe (Zelstone) from two black parents, Neptune and Duchess. Ben's background was all black. It was in 1908 that a yellow was first successful in winning a place in a field trial. The Knaith kennel, owned by Mrs Veronica Wormald, was another very famous early 'yellow' kennel, established in

about 1910. After World War One, the colour became much more readily accepted. At one point Mrs Wormald took one of her yellow dogs to be shown at Crufts, then held at the old Crystal Palace. She was told by the steward that Golden Retrievers were in another ring. Mrs Wormald was far from pleased but she got her own back, winning third place with her yellow Labrador in a Labrador class. Mrs Wormald went on to breed one of the few Dual Champions, Knaith Banjo, in Britain and developed a very distinctive kennel. I was fortunate to meet Mrs Wormald when I started in the breed as a child. Looking back on that day, she paid a huge compliment to the breeder of my first bitch, Mary Rider (Redvales), by

watching my efforts in the ring and then summoning me to her side and asking if she could buy my bitch. Can you imagine it? I said "no" – I didn't quite appreciate who I was saying no to!

BREED RECOGNITION

In 1903 the Kennel Club recognised the Labrador as a breed in its own right in response to its growing popularity. Labrador pups could be registered as such, but many pups were registered as Labradors who were, in fact, Labrador crosses. If the results of retriever cross litters looked like

Labrador puppies, their owners could register them as Labradors. Ironically, in Newfoundland, the original St John's Dog was becoming increasingly rare.
In 1916, The Labrador Retriever Club was founded by Mrs Quintin Dick (Banchory), the Hon. Arthur Holland-Hibbert (Munden) and a group of influential Labrador owners. The formation of the club came about following a dispute at Crufts. The previous year, a black dog called Horton Max, owned by Mr A. Shuter, had won the Challenge Certificate at Crufts. Max was a good example of the breed, yet he is recorded as being sired by a

Flat Coated Retriever named Beechgrove Peter. Indeed, a close relative of his, owned by Reginald Crooke, had also been successful at Crufts, but in the Flat Coated Retriever ring. Labrador owners felt this was wrong, and so they sent a petition to the Kennel Club, requesting that only pure Labradors could enter Labrador classes at shows. The Kennel Club agreed to this and opened a separate register for interbred (retriever crosses) dogs. This meant that Labradors could be registered as pure Labradors, and supposedly nothing else. At the formation of the club Mrs Quintin Dick was appointed secretary and treasurer, a position she held for 19 years, and the Hon. Arthur Holland-Hibbert was elected chairman. The committee included: Lord Chesterfield, Lord Lonsdale, Lord Vivian, Lord Harlech, Mr Burdett-Coutts MP, Mrs R. Heaton and Mr A. Nichol. They drew up a Breed Standard, which was accepted by the Kennel Club.

The aim of the club was to protect the development of the purebred Labrador. By 1920 questions were being asked as to what really constituted a purebred Labrador Retriever; it was decided that a dog registered as a Labrador, but who had one parent of another breed e.g. a Flat Coat, was not eligible for club special awards. However, when this first generation cross was mated to a Labrador, his/her progeny would be eligible for the club specials.

The breed quickly became more popular. Registrations in 1912 were 281, but by 1922 they reached 916. In the early days of the club much help was given to gamekeeper members in order to encourage them to show their working dogs. They were eligible for reduced fees, special awards and even financial help in trialling their own dogs.

A lovely black bitch, Ch. Liddly Cornflower, has been used for The Labrador Retriever Club logo for many years.

In 1925 the Yellow Labrador Club was formed, with the aims of protecting the breed, providing classes at shows, and running field trials. The club today runs an Open show purely for yellows, and has an Open yellow class for dogs and bitches at its Championship show.

As a measure of merit, titles (Field Trial Champion, Champion, Show Champion) in the field and in the show ring have always been much valued. The only major change in either has been when the title of Show Champion (Sh. Ch.) was allowed from 1958 onwards. Before that, a dog could only become Champion if he/she had won three Challenge Certificates (CCs) under three different judges (in more recent times at least one of those CCs must have be won when the dog is over 12 months), and had either gained a field trial award, or a Show Gundog Working Certificate. If a dog did not have working certification, he could not claim the title of Champion, regardless of how many CCs he had won. However, the title that proves most elusive is Dual Champion, going to a dog that gains both Field Trial Champion and Champion titles. In the history of the breed, in Britain, only 10 dogs have succeeded in doing this.

Ch. Liddy Cornflower: Featured as the logo for the Labrador Retriever Club.

DUAL CHAMPIONS

- Dual Ch. Banchory Bolo (born 1915), black male, by Scandal of Glynn x Caerhowell Nettle. Breeder: Major Banner. Owner: Lorna, Countess Howe.
- Dual Ch. Banchory Sunspeck (born 1917), black male, by Ch. Ilderton Ben x Dungavel Juniper. Breeder: J. Alexander. Owner: Lorna, Countess Howe.
- Dual Ch. Titus of Whitmore (born 1919), black male, by Twist of Whitmore x Teale of Whitmore. Breeder/owner: Mr Twyford.
- Dual Ch. Flute of Flodden (born 1922), black male, by Dual Ch. Titus of Whitmore x Wemyss Rachel. Breeder: Mr A. Campbell. Owner: Lord Joicey.
- Dual Ch. Bramshaw Bob (born 1929), black male, by Ch. Ingleston Ben x Bramshaw Brimble. Breeder: Mrs Sofer Whitburn. Owner: Sir George Thursby Bt. and Lorna, Countess Howe.
- Dual Ch. Banchory Painter (born 1930), black male, by Peter the Painter x Glenhead Bess. Breeder J. Annand. Owner: Lorna, Countess Howe.
- Dual Ch. Lochar Nessie (born 1933), black bitch, by Lochar Peter x Lochar Biddy. Breeder: Mr T. Dinwoodie. Owner: Mrs Morris.
- Dual Ch. Staindrop Saighdear (born 1944), yellow male, by Glenhead Jimmy x Our Lil. Breeder: Mr J. Murray Dewar. Owner: Mr E. Winter.
- Dual Ch. Rockstead Footspark (born 1945), black male, by Ludford Razor x Jaaia. Breeder Major J. Benson. Owner: R. MacDonald.
- Dual Ch. Knaith Banjo (born 1946), yellow male, by Poppleton Golden Russet x Knaith Brilliantine. Breeder/owner: Mrs V. Wormald.

Dual Ch. Bramshaw Bob: One of only 10 Labradors to become a Dual Champion.

The great Banchory Bolo: A bad'un who earned his place in history as a Dual Champion and influential sire.

BANCHORY BOLO

Dual Champion Banchory Bolo is probably the most famous of all Labradors. Born in 1915 he came to Countess Howe as a two-year old, sired by her own Scandal of Glynn. He had been through the hands of several trainers, who could do nothing with him. By all accounts he was in poor condition when he arrived at Liverpool Street Station and was wearing a muzzle due his disagreeable temperament.

Upon arriving at his new home, his chain and muzzle were removed, whereupon it took an hour to catch and kennel him. Soon after this, Bolo became seriously ill, which may have been a blessing in disguise.

The Countess nursed him devotedly, and Bolo grew to trust a human being, perhaps for the first time. As time went by he was taken out shooting where he showed his natural abilities as a retriever of birds, but on ground game he could not contain himself. However, training by harsh means was never going to work with this dog, and so more suitable methods had to be used for him.

Things were going well until a stable boy cracked a whip near Bolo, causing him to take flight, jumping a high gate with spiked railings. In the early hours of the following morning he found his way home, and took himself to his basket in the Countess's room. It was then discovered

that he had been badly injured by the spikes on the gate. He was stitched up by the kennel-man and, in time, he recovered.

A year later he gained his Field title and then went on to gain his title in the show ring to become the first Dual Champion in the breed – quite a feat for a dog who had been regarded as a rogue and a bad'un. With limited use as a stud dog, Bolo still had a great influence on the breed. Bolo also left his mark, quite literally, on the breed in another way. Today we occasionally see white hairs or patches on the back of the front legs, just above the feet. Not to be confused with the white hairs under the feet, these hairs are known as 'Bolo marks' and are highly prized.

THE GREAT DIVIDE

It is unlikely that there will be any more Dual Champions, due to a split in the breed. This has gradually happened for a number of reasons. The Labrador is no longer purely a working dog who is judged by his abilities. As a result of his wonderful, easygoing nature, he has become the most popular breed in many countries, living alongside us as a family pet. This means that dogs and bitches have been bred from with gradually changing temperaments and physical features.

Two extremes of this are the competitive field trial dogs, who are of a lighter build than the original dogs, and, in many cases, do not possess the features required in the Breed Standard (the blueprint for the breed). Points such as otter-like tails for use as a rudder; correct, dense, water- and weather-resistant coats; and the general conformation that enables the dog to move about with the minimum of effort and least amount of stress

A working Labrador has a more athletic build than Labradors bred from show lines.

on bones, joints and ligaments, are not featured highly in the breeding of field trial dogs.

The show type of Labrador has become somewhat heavier and more stockily built over the years. Many of them are not given the opportunity to show if they are capable of doing the job that the breed was originally bred for, and it is impossible to know how much of the instinct is still there in dogs that are shown but not worked. Most Labradors will pick up things around the home, but that is a long way from displaying if they would really make good retrievers in the field. There is no way of knowing if they would be gun-shy, hard-mouthed or have the biddable temperament that is so receptive to training.

In the middle of this divide, there are a number of breeders who still strive to conform to the Breed Standard while also producing a dog that is capable of being a good shooting companion and picking-up dog.

It is hard to tell if show dogs still retain the working instincts of their ancestors, but given the opportunity it is likely that many will do.

Am Ch. Boli of Blake: Awarded Best of Breed at the first American Specialty Show in 1932.

Dual Ch. Shed of Arden: Sired by an imported British dog, Ch. Raffles of Earlsmore.

THE LABRADOR IN AMERICA

Just as in the UK, the early imported Labradors into America were classified as simply Retrievers, alongside other known Retrievers. They were imported from Britain in a small way before World War One, and were used as gundogs by several wealthy Long Islanders who were keen to shoot in the English style. These American enthusiasts had visited shooting estates in Britain, and had arranged for gamekeepers, guns and dogs to be imported into America.

In 1917 the first Labrador was registered: she was Brocklehirst Nell, and she came from Munden bloodlines. The American Kennel Club gave official recognition to the Labrador Retriever in the 1920s, and the American Labrador Retriever Club was formed in 1931. The first Specialty show (a show held for one breed only) was held in 1933 with 34 entries. The judge was

Mrs Marshall Field (the first president of the club 1931-1935) and her Best of Breed was Boli of Blake, born in 1932 (Ch. Ingleston Ben x Banchory Trace). He was bred by Lady Howe but whelped in the United States and owned by Franklin B. Lord. Boli later became the first bench Champion (Champion in the show ring).

In 1935 Jay F. Carlisle became the new president. His Wingan kennels, on Long Island, was a major influence on the breed in its early days, and his stock was the foundation for a number of influential kennels. Some of his early imports from Britain were from the Drinkstone and Banchory kennels; the most important being Drinkstone Peg. Peg was in whelp to the famous Dual Champion Bramshaw Bob, and from this litter came a number of title-holders.

Another very well-known import, bought by Dr Samuel Millbank, was Champion Raffles

of Earlsmore. He gained his title in a very short time, and was also a successful sire. His best-known progeny were from a litter out of Field Trial Champion Decoy of Arden (Odds On – Peggy of Shipton). In this litter were the Dual Champions Braes, Gorse, and Shed of Arden. It also contained Champion Earlsmoor Moor of Arden, who went to live with his sire's owner, Dr Millbank. This dog had a spectacular show career and was the first Labrador to win Best in Show at all-breed shows in the United States. The mating was so successful that it was repeated and, yet again, it produced some top winners. Decoy and her brother, Blind of Arden, became the first bitch and dog field trial title-holders in the breed. Michael of Glenmere (Ace of Whitmore – Vixen of Glenmere) became the first American Dual Champion Labrador, owned by Mr Goelet.

In the 1980s Richard Wolters, an author, travelled from America to Newfoundland in search of any original 'Water Dogs' that might still be alive. In a small fishing village, only accessible by boat, he found what seemed to be the last of them: two black males with white on their feet and chest, just as can still be seen occasionally today. They were brothers from different litters. As there seemed to be no Water Dog bitches left in Newfoundland, after many years of searching, these males seemed to be the very last two representatives of the breed. The close ancestors of these two old dogs had worked on the local boats. Fishing was carried out on long lines, which had a number of hooks on them. If a fish detached itself from a hook, the dogs would jump into the freezing water and retrieve the fish back to the boats. The dogs needed no training; they just

knew what to do. When the owner of these dogs was asked why they were no longer used for fishing, the only reason given was that the hooks had been improved and so the fish did not escape as they had done before.

MODERN TIMES

Registrations have risen steadily over the years and the Labrador Retriever is now the most popular breed of dog throughout the world. Unfortunately, not all puppies are registered, and so the true figures for Labrador puppies born each year is much higher. This degree of popularity is not necessarily good for the breed. Many years ago, most Labradors would have been working dogs, but as time has moved on, more and more Labs have become family pets. This, in itself, is not a bad thing, but it reduces the

means of proving that the breed is true to its original type and purpose. An increase in the number of pups born also brings problems in finding suitable homes, and so we see far more dogs going through 'rescue' and having to be rehomed. There has also been a rise in the number of commercial 'kennels'. These 'kennels' do not have the good of the breed at heart, nor do they make use of the various tests we have available to reduce the incidence of hereditary diseases.

Despite these challenges, the Labrador, for the most part, still retains the character, temperament and instinct of those first dogs that sailed into Poole harbour. Then, as now, the Labrador is prized for his easygoing nature and biddability; the Lab is here to serve us, and he is always happy to do so.

The Labrador's outstanding temperament remains the breed's greatest asset.

A LABRADOR FOR YOUR LIFESTYLE

Chapter 3

There have been many books written over the years about the Labrador Retriever. Perhaps the reason for the breed's popularity is that they are considered by the general public to be the ideal 'family dog'. The introduction to the Labrador Retriever in the Kennel Club's *Book of Breed Standards* states that the Labrador is one of the best all-round dogs in the world. It goes on to say that the Labrador is considered a real gentleman, adores children, and has a kind, loving nature and a confident air. These words confirm what Labrador owners worldwide already know: the Labrador is a very special breed of dog.

Unfortunately, this also makes the Labrador very vulnerable to puppy farmers, who breed puppies purely for monetary gain, and this is a subject which is of constant concern to responsible breeders all over the world. The main reason for raising this at the start of this chapter is that it is one of the most important issues that we have to face in our breed today. These wonderful dogs are clearly being bred in their thousands by unscrupulous breeders who care nothing for the welfare of the breed.

It is very easy to see why people find a seven-week-old Labrador puppy adorable. However, these bundles of fun do not stay as cute and endearing puppies for long, but grow up into large, adult dogs who need adequate exercise, good-quality feeding and appropriate socialisation during development. Human contact is essential to ensure a well-rounded Lab. By far the first and most important factor to consider before deciding to buy any animal, especially a dog, is what kind of life you will be able to offer him.

We have all seen the stickers displayed on the back of cars that emphasise that a dog is not just for Christmas but for a lifetime. As an animal lover, I feel that the decision to own a dog is one of the most important you can ever make, because it involves being responsible for a life, albeit one with four legs and a tail. It comes next in line to getting married, having a child, choosing a career or buying a home. If you think this is a ridiculous comparison, then buy a goldfish as a pet.

I would urge anyone thinking about buying a Labrador to answer honestly a number of questions before making the commitment. For that is exactly what it is: a commitment, which could last for 16-plus years.

QUESTIONS TO ASK

- **Does my lifestyle allow me to have a Labrador as a pet and a companion?**
Please think about this very carefully. The majority of Labradors who end up in

rescue organisations are those who have been bought on a whim without due consideration to owner lifestyle, work or family commitments. Many are bought by young couples who have decided to set up home together. Unfortunately, in many cases the relationship breaks down and the dog ends up in rescue or back with the breeder. Although the owners have loved and looked after the dog very well, their circumstances have changed and neither one is in a position to continue to look after the dog on their own.

Many couples decide to buy a Labrador when they get married. It might seem to some a ludicrous comparison to make, but a dog is often seen as an early substitute for a child. It could be possibly misconstrued as a way of showing commitment to the relationship – but with one big difference. It is easier to find the dog a new home if the marriage breaks down. Consequently rehoming dogs from broken marriages is a problem involving all breeds and rescue societies.

• **Can I afford not only to buy a Labrador puppy but to feed him for approximately 16 years?**
Some people might only consider short-term costs, i.e. the cost of the puppy and his inoculations. But the cost of keeping a dog is ongoing, and by far the largest outlay is feeding, as it is essential to give your Labrador a top-quality, well-balanced diet throughout his life.

• **Have I enough space in my home?**
From the very earliest days of the breed, the Labrador was bred and developed for country pursuits, and he remains a bit of a country squire at heart. The big city is not really his scene. While it is true that the Labrador loves nothing better than to run in the field or in the wood, not everyone who aspires to having a Labrador can boast ownership of a country house and estate. A Labrador is a medium-sized dog who will require a fair degree of space within your home. Taking on any seven-week-old puppy is like bringing a child into your home, and, like a growing child, your Labrador will need more room as he gets older.

A flat or an apartment is not a suitable place for a Labrador to live. Believe me, sharing a flat with a dog the size of a Labrador would be like living with a baby elephant. A good breeder will emphasise that a puppy must not climb up and down stairs, as this can damage growing bones and joints. If you want a dog and live in a

38

flat or apartment, buy a Chihuahua, which is easy to carry up and down stairs.

- **Is my garden of adequate size, and is it escape-proof?**
For the first few months, your puppy will be able to exercise quite adequately in your garden, but the garden has to be big enough to allow him to run around without causing himself any injury. One of the worst injuries I have seen in a young puppy was caused by him running into an old washing pole in the owner's garden.

There are also a lot of plants that are poisonous to animals, and therefore you need to make sure your garden is free from anything potentially dangerous.

Your local garden centre should be able to give you all the information you need on poisonous plants. The internet is also a great source of information on this subject.

Your garden must also be escape-proof unless you are very fortunate and have eyes in the back of your head. Like young children, puppies are very inquisitive by nature. I have known some puppies who were undoubtedly related to Houdini. One owner spent over three weeks trying to find out how his puppy kept escaping from his garden. He finally managed to solve the puzzle by sitting in the garden for hours and watching his puppy play. There were a number of bushes at the back of his garden, and,

unknown to him, the pup had dug a hole around one that was situated close to the fence. I don't think the owner could quite believe the small space the puppy was able to squeeze himself through. So be warned!

- **Can I afford to give my Labrador the best veterinary care for approximately 16 years?**
If you are extremely lucky, your dog will not require a great deal of veterinary treatment during his life, but routine care (such as worming, boosters, teeth cleaning and nail care) will mean an expensive visit to the vet's. A reputable breeder will always recommend pet insurance, and six weeks' free insurance will

A small Labrador puppy will grow into a medium-sized, energetic dog. Do you have enough room in your home?

normally be included in your puppy pack. Prices of pet insurance vary depending on the company you insure with and the type of cover provided, but it is well worth continuing to insure your puppy as a safeguard against a large veterinary bill.

When choosing a veterinary practice, try to go on personal recommendation. Another important consideration is whether the practice offers a 24-hour service or whether out-of-hours calls are referred to a practice further away.

- **Can I afford to pay for boarding kennel fees when I am on holiday?**
Most families take more than one holiday a year, and if you are not planning to take your dog with you, boarding can be an expensive outlay. Again, shop around to find the best boarding kennels in your area; you can also ask your veterinary practice for a recommendation. Choosing a good boarding kennel can be the difference between your dog being well cared for, or simply fed and locked up for the duration of your holiday. I would suggest you visit the boarding kennel well in advance of you making a booking so you can meet the staff and view the facilities. Most boarding kennels love Labradors, as they are normally very easy to deal with: they eat well, they are good-natured, and they usually adapt quite well to kennel life.

- **What if my circumstances change and I have to go back to work/increase my work hours?**
It may be that, over the years, your circumstances will change due to working commitments, or you may decide to go back to work after having children. It could mean that you have to consider employing the services of a pet sitter, a professional dog walker, or you may wish to put your Labrador in doggy day care, where he can be looked after in someone else's home. Again, a recommendation is always the best policy. After all, this person will be responsible for the care of your Labrador. Please take care that you employ the right person for both your family and your dog. I have seen this arrangement work out admirably for all concerned, but it can also be a disaster if you do not give it due care and consideration.

- **Have I the time and, more importantly, the patience to train a Labrador puppy?**
Your puppy will only be well trained if you are prepared to spend time every day training him. You also need patience and understanding. Training should always be fun and although your dog should respect you, he should never be frightened or show signs of stress during training. It is a good plan to join a dog training club where you can socialise your puppy and get him used to being with other dogs. You can find a training club in your area by

Do you have the time and patience to train a puppy?

recommendation from your vet, by talking to other doggy friends, or by contacting your local council and speaking to a dog warden.

- **Am I prepared to monitor my puppy's exercise, adhering to the breeder's guidelines, during the first few months?**
Exercise should be carefully controlled while a Labrador puppy is growing. The musculoskeletal system changes constantly throughout life, but these changes are most rapid during the first few months of puppyhood and slow with maturity (which is about 12 months in a Labrador) The skeletal system is most susceptible to physical abuse during the first six months; the signs may be lameness and/or altered growth, and both can affect the soundness of adult dogs.

Obviously, you will need to give your puppy some exercise during the vulnerable growing period. He will need to be collar- and lead-trained, and he will need to be socialised, becoming accustomed to the noise of traffic and a variety of everyday situations. This can be achieved on a short walk twice a day. Your garden can be used for free exercise, as we

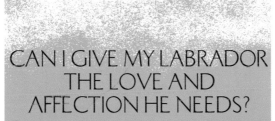

CAN I GIVE MY LABRADOR THE LOVE AND AFFECTION HE NEEDS?

Labradors need human company; by their very nature, they are people dogs. No matter how big a welcome your Labrador gives you when you return home, you need to bear in mind that he will be stressed if he is left on his own for long periods of time. Labradors get bored very quickly, and, when they are young, boredom leads to chewing.

A Labrador needs to be stimulated, and the best way to do this is for the dog to be around people as much as possible. A Labrador will take as much love and attention as you are prepared to give him, but he will become less demanding as he matures and will be happy to lie at your feet.

have already established that it is secure and free from potential hazards. Your puppy should never be allowed to exhaust himself. When he is tired, he will lie down and rest. Never try to force exercise on him by walking him for long distances. Unlike a child, who would simply put the brakes on if he/she is tired, a puppy will continue to walk until he is completely exhausted. How many times have you seen someone in the street drag a young puppy

behind them when all the puppy wants to do is sit down? Think of your puppy as a very young child. Would you ask a toddler to walk for a mile? Exercise should be kept to a minimum for the first six months of his life. Your Labrador will have plenty of time to run around when he has finished growing, so please be patient.

LABRADORS AND CHILDREN
If you already have children, a Labrador puppy will be a delightful addition to your family. To get relationships off to a good start, it is important to see the world from a puppy's perspective, and also to ensure that your children learn to respect the puppy. Here are a few tips gained over the years from both personal experience and the experience of friends and new owners.

- You must set ground rules before the puppy arrives in your home and stick to them, no matter how many times the children may plead or cajole you. The most important of these is that the puppy should *never ever be left alone with a child*, no matter what age that child may be.

- Children, by their very nature, are born to shout, scream, cry,

Children and puppies can be a magical mix, but it is essential to lay down some ground rules.

and run around all of their waking hours. A puppy, by his very nature, has learned to fight and bite his littermates, squeal, bark and run around all of his waking hours. However, a puppy grows at a very rapid rate, and will need more rest during the day. Please bear this in mind.

• The puppy, like the young child, does not know right from wrong. A puppy may be extremely daring and believe that any obstacle put in his path is there to eat, chew, climb on, or leap off.

• A puppy will eat anything that remotely looks or smells like food, and even if an item doesn't smell of food, he will still want to put it in his mouth.

• A puppy has no morals when it comes to nipping or biting; he thinks it is a game – the very same game he played with his littermates. *You* have to discourage play-biting.

• More importantly, a puppy definitely cannot read, so don't expect him to know that the bottle under the sink or in the utility/laundry room is dangerous. A puppy doesn't have a clue that the bottle that looks so good rolling around the floor contains something that might burn or poison him.

• In the garden, a puppy thinks that all the plants, bushes and trees can be eaten, and that every container or puddle that has liquid in it can be drunk from.

• A simple misunderstanding on either the dog or child's part can end in disaster.

• A child should never be allowed to lift or carry the puppy.

• A child should never be allowed to take the puppy walking. A young child has no accurate sense of balance and the puppy can easily pull them over, or the lead can tangle around the child's legs or the dog's legs. Worse still, the puppy and/or child can end up on the road.

• Children's toys are a great source of amusement for a puppy. A pup can chew and shred soft toys and socks in minutes. Hard items, such as mobile phones, cars, toy soldiers and books, are like dog bones to puppies, and they can crunch and chew them up in less time than you could possibly imagine. Small things, such as marbles and stones, can be swallowed and will require an operation to retrieve.

• Electric cables on lamps, televisions and vacuum cleaners are another source of amusement. It only takes seconds for you to have a dead puppy.

• Children should never be allowed to feed the puppy. The puppy will become accustomed to taking things from the child and cannot differentiate between something he is allowed to eat and something he should not have.

• Children should never be allowed to disturb the puppy while he is eating. Some dogs can be aggressive while they are eating and it is the quickest way for a child to be bitten. The dog is not at fault, as he sees the child simply as a littermate who is trying to steal his food.

• The puppy's crate should be his sanctuary (see Chapter 4 for information on indoor kennels). The puppy will retreat to his 'own space' when he wants to sleep or be on his own. Please ensure that he is not disturbed. Some children see the crate as a toy to crawl into. This should never be

Food can be a contentious issue, so it is better to keep a puppy out of temptation's way.

allowed, regardless of whether the puppy is in or out of his crate. Children should also be stopped from trying to wake up the puppy by poking their fingers in the crate and prodding him.

• Do not allow a child and puppy to play chase. Again, the puppy sees the child simply as a littermate and will try to catch the child's clothing. This may lead to the child being nipped, clothes

being torn, or the child falling over and injuring the puppy.

• A play nip from a puppy can be quite vicious, and a young pup will try to bite, scratch or nip at every opportunity until he has learnt to inhibit this reaction (see Chapter 4).

• Please make sure the puppy is corrected for any misdemeanour in the same way you would correct a child. Make it clear that his

It takes an expert eye to work out if a puppy has the potential to develop into a top-quality show dog.

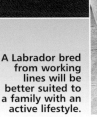

A Labrador bred from working lines will be better suited to a family with an active lifestyle.

behaviour is undesirable, by saying "No" in a firm voice; if he has hold of a 'forbidden' item, substitute it with one of his own toys.

This may be a great deal to take on board, but most of it is straightforward common sense. Just remember: there is little difference between the rearing of young children and young puppies, but unfortunately, some of the time they do not mix well.

FINDING A BREEDER
The best place to buy a Labrador puppy is from a reputable breeder, who you can find by contacting a breed club. Most breed clubs will not allow anyone who has not carried out the necessary clearances of hips,

elbows and eyes to be placed on their puppy register. The Kennel Club and the American Kennel Club also run a puppy referral service on their websites (see page 152). It is important to be aware of the different types of breeder before making your choice. Please ask questions and visit many kennels. You will only then begin to see the marked differences in the condition and environment in which puppies are kept.

THE SHOW KENNEL
This type of breeder will exhibit their dogs at competition level, and their aim is to produce quality Labradors for the show ring. When breeding puppies, temperament and conformation will be high on the list of

priorities. A quality show puppy will be well bodied, and have good bone and substance. The male dogs will be slightly broader in the head than the females. The temperament will be very outgoing, with an eager-to-please attitude. Most show breeders are looking to improve their stock for the show ring, and will probably be breeding with the intention of keeping a puppy for themselves. A successful show kennel might have a waiting list of people who want puppies for the show ring, but it is worth bearing in mind that not all the puppies in a litter will have the attributes necessary. Therefore, if you are looking for a quality pet puppy, you would be well advised to place your name on their waiting list.

THE WORKING KENNEL

This type of breeder is predominantly breeding to produce Labradors to compete in field trial competition or to be a working gundog. Breeders of 'working' Labradors are looking for a dog of sound temperament, who is agile and fast over the ground, who can be trained to obey the whistle, and who will be capable of using his nose to find and retrieve game. A successful field trial kennel might have a waiting list of people for puppies, but again, it is worth bearing in mind that not all the puppies in the litter will have the desired qualities for the field. If you place your name on a waiting list, you may be lucky enough to get a puppy. The field trial puppy will be lighter framed than the show puppy, to allow him to quarter ground at a fast pace. He will probably be smaller in stature and will also have less bone and substance than the show puppy. He should have an excellent temperament and be of a happy disposition. Many believe a field trial bred puppy will have a higher energy level, and will therefore require owners with an active lifestyle.

THE PET BREEDER

This person will have bred a litter from their pet Labrador and might not consider themselves to be a breeder as such. The reason for breeding a litter may well be because the owner wants a puppy from a much-loved pet. Sometimes, a pet owner believes it is better for a bitch to have a litter before she is spayed. I have seen a good few litters over the

THE PUPPY FARMER

By and large, a puppy farmer is everything a responsible breeder is not. In many cases, a number of breeds will be produced at the same establishment, although I have known puppy farmers who specialise in Labradors because they are easy sellers. A puppy farmer cares little for the welfare of the stock bred or reared; the motive for breeding puppies is purely financial.

Generally, little thought or planning goes into matching a suitable dog and bitch, and the unfortunate bitch may be mated season after season. This will continue without respite until she is beyond the age of producing puppies, whereupon she will be discarded. A puppy farmer will not consider the temperament of the puppies, and will rarely let you see the parents of the puppies offered for sale.

Be wary of claims that the puppies are registered. Anyone can register pups with their national Kennel Club if they have KC registered parents, and many puppy farmers do. This may be one of the problems, as people see Kennel Club registered puppies in an advert and consider it an automatic sign of quality – which it is not. Although a puppy farmer will be more than happy to take your money, he/she will fail to offer sound advice about the breed, and will not take the puppy back if you should encounter problems with your puppy's health or temperament, or should your circumstances change. Obviously, you want nothing to do with this type of breeder.

The best plan is to go to a reputable breeder who has established their own line of typical-looking Labradors.

years from owners who have only wanted one litter from their bitch, but have taken sound advice and have reared a lovely litter of puppies. Hopefully, the stud dog owner will have helped out, making the novice breeder aware of all the necessary health checks, such as eye tests, plus hip and elbow scoring. If you are buying from this 'breeder', please ensure that health checks have been carried out on both the sire and the dam of the litter. (For more information on hereditary conditions, see Chapter 8.) You may be lucky and buy a nice pet dog from this type of breeder, but the chances of getting exactly what you want are considerably lower than if you go to a professional breeder who has established their own breeding line. It is always better to seek advice from a breed club in your area before going to view a litter. Most breed clubs will have a puppy register and will give you valuable help and guidance.

YELLOW, BLACK OR CHOCOLATE?

I have never quite understood why colour is so important to people when they are looking for a Labrador puppy. However, arguably it may well be the deciding factor as to whether someone buys a puppy or not.

I should think that the biggest percentage of puppies bred in the UK and USA over the last 20 years have been yellow. However, over the last 10 years or so, the breeding of chocolate puppies has increased dramatically. It is all a matter of fashion, and, at the present time, the most 'wanted' colour is chocolate. Consequently, puppy farmers have caught on to this lucrative market and are breeding chocolate puppies in abundance. They are also asking ridiculous prices for them. From a buyer's perspective, it is important to ask any breeder why they have bred a litter.

Whether your preference is black, yellow or chocolate, a Labrador is a Labrador in any colour. There should be no difference in temperament or construction, and definitely none in the aptitude to be either a show, working, or field trial dog. However, I have yet to see a chocolate Field Trial Champion in the UK, but perhaps it is just a matter of time. If you are choosing a pet dog, colour is of absolutely no importance, beyond personal preference. Temperament should be considered a top priority.

Yellow, chocolate or black – the choice is yours...

MALE OR FEMALE?

Again, this is the choice of the individual, but by far the main reason for people choosing a male is because they do not want the problem of a female coming into season every six months. However, it has to be remembered that a male is potentially 'in season' 12 months a year, and is capable of mating a bitch at any time, whereas a female is only in danger of being mated at two six-month intervals.

If your Labrador is bought as a family pet and you have no intention of breeding, it is a good idea to spay/castrate your dog. Many veterinary surgeons will suggest that a Labrador is neutered at a very early age, but in my experience, it is preferable if a female has one season, and the male should reach at least 12 months of age. This is only my personal opinion, but most breeders would agree that the dog should reach a reasonable degree of maturity before neutering takes place.

Whether you choose a male or a female, the most important priority should be that of temperament. In Labradors, the temperament should not vary between male and female, and buying from a reputable breeder should provide you with the comfort of knowing that this has also been at the top of their list of priorities.

WHAT TO EXPECT

As a potential puppy buyer, you must consider that you are purchasing a companion for the next 16 years. If you are careful in your selection of breeder, you will dramatically increase the chances of owning a healthy, happy companion, rather than an expensive, stressful drain on your finances and emotions.

The most important factor in determining your puppy's health, looks and temperament is the puppy's parentage. All reputable breeders put a great deal of thought into breeding a litter of puppies. A breeder must not only consider matching the parents, based on their health checks, but on whether the mating of one dog to another will improve their stock and produce a quality litter. From a breeder's perspective, the most important reason for breeding a bitch is to continue their line. The breeder may wish to keep one of the litter to exhibit in the show ring, perhaps for the field, or to improve the quality of their stock.

It is a mistaken belief that a buyer should be able to see both parents when they view a litter. A breeder seeking to improve their stock will probably have used a stud dog owned by another breeder, and so it is not always possible to see both parents in the breeder's own kennel. If a breeder uses a stud dog from another kennel, you can be confident that they are striving to improve the quality of their stock rather than breeding for profit. Conversely, I do know of a number of established breeders who use their own stud dogs, but these are always used because they are considered to be the best match for their bitches, and not simply as a matter of convenience. However, you should always be able to see the mother of the puppies, and if you are unable to do so for any reason, I would advise you to

The male (yellow) is a bigger, more powerful animal than the female, but there is little difference in temperament.

VIEWING THE LITTER

It is important to see the mother with her puppies.

The puppies should be kept in a clean, hygienic environment.

think twice about buying from the breeder.

Another significant factor that will affect your puppy's future is how the litter has been reared. Many breeders will set up a whelping box in their home, where the puppies are born and will usually spend the first few weeks of their lives. Labrador puppies grow at an alarming rate, and, when they are old enough (around four weeks of age), they will normally be moved outside into a puppy kennel. Puppies need lots of human contact during the first few weeks of their lives, so it goes without saying that the environment in

which a puppy is reared is very important. Breeders may utilise a wide variety of facilities for puppy raising, from elaborate kennel buildings to garages or living rooms, but cleanliness and human contact is what is important.

VIEWING A LITTER

So, you have taken all the advice, made your decision, and have arranged to go and view a litter of puppies. What should you be looking for?

• The puppies should be well socialised, outgoing and friendly, with no sign of stress

or nervousness. All areas where the puppies and other dogs are kept should be clean, and their surroundings should be safe and well maintained.

• The breeder will have started a worming programme for the puppies, beginning at three weeks of age and then at fortnightly intervals.

• There is no magic age for separating a pup from his littermates and dam. However, there is significant evidence that suggests a puppy should not leave the breeder before seven weeks.

The breeder will have had time to observe the puppies and will know their individual personalities.

- You should be given instructions regarding the care and feeding of your puppy well in advance of taking the puppy home. This should come in the form of a diet sheet detailing the feeding programme for your puppy for the next 12 months.

- You should receive a contract, which must clearly state the conditions of sale (see Chapter 4: The New Arrival).

- You should be given advice on the amount of exercise to give your puppy. This is fundamental to the development of your puppy and should be clear and precise. The consequences can be dire if a puppy's exercise is not controlled.

You should always be able to access friendly follow-up advice from the puppy's breeder. Conscientious and caring breeders love to hear from the new owners of their puppies. In fact, some owners phone me on their dog's birthday, simply to keep in touch and let me know that they could never see themselves with any other breed than a Labrador.

THE NEW ARRIVAL

Chapter 4

Y ou have chosen to own a Labrador, the most popular breed of pedigree dog in the United Kingdom and in North America. What is the secret of the Labrador's phenomenal success? Labs are happy, healthy, companionable dogs, who love human company, and food; they are intelligent, placid, easily trained and easy to care for. Best of all, the Labrador has a fun-loving, loyal temperament. If you look after your Labrador properly, you can look forward to many years of close companionship.

Obviously, you want life with your Labrador to get off to a good start, so make time to prepare your home for the new arrival. This is vital if you are bringing a puppy home, but it is also important if you are rehoming an adult Labrador, who will not be familiar with your house or garden.

PREPARATIONS OUTSIDE

FENCING AND SECURITY

Make sure the garden is well fenced. Labradors are intelligent, inquisitive dogs, who are usually thinking one step ahead of you. The last thing you want is your Lab finding a hole in the boundary fence and escaping across the road or into the garden next door within the first few minutes of arrival.

Labradors can clear medium-height fences quite easily, if they are so inclined. Your garden should be enclosed by a fence that is at least a 5-6ft high (1.5 to 1.8 metres); the fence should be close boarded or made of sturdy

Make sure your Labrador is safe and secure in a well-fenced garden.

IN THE GARDEN

Select a designated toilet area for your Labrador to use in the garden. This will help with house training (see page 65), and it also makes cleaning up easier.

There may be a time when you want to erect an outdoor kennel and run if you have sufficient space. Check out the garden, and decide on the best location.

A fenced outdoor exercise run will keep your Labrador where you want him to be....

wire netting on post and rails. Strong close-boarded fencing is the best. If you opt for wire, choose galvanized stock fencing on strong posts, concreted into the ground. It is better not to use chain link fencing, as Labradors can pull and chew it, making it look horribly messy, rather like unravelled knitting.

If you have a high, wrought-iron side-gate to your back garden, make sure the gaps at the bottom, and between the vertical bars, are covered with wire up to 3ft (90 cm) high, otherwise a puppy will be able to squeeze underneath, or through the bars, and escape. The same applies to a high, wooden side-gate; ensure the puppy cannot get under the bottom rail. Ideally, garden gates should be fitted with sturdy bolts on the garden side, so no one can accidentally open the gate from outside, allowing the dog to escape.

POTENTIAL HAZARDS

Search the ground for broken glass, bits of wood with nails sticking out, broken manhole covers or other dangerous objects. Make sure there are no electrical cables, at a height where they could be chewed.

If there is a greenhouse in a prominent central position, put temporary low-level wooden boarding across the exposed glass sides. An exuberant Labrador charging around in play is more than capable of crashing through the glass when he is not watching where he is going.

Remove children's abandoned toys from lawns, patios and decking, otherwise they may well be chewed up or swallowed. (The children might not like their toys ruined either!)

Surround your ornamental fishponds with wire netting, otherwise you will find your Labrador in there, swimming with the goldfish! Although the adult Labrador will enjoy taking a dip and be able to get out of the pond, a puppy could drown if he falls in when unsupervised; if he cannot climb up the vertical sides of the pool to get out, he will quickly tire. The same applies to an outdoor swimming pool, even if it is protected with a pool cover – fence it off completely!

Ensure the garden shed is firmly shut and that any dangerous chemicals stored inside are on shelves at a high level beyond a Labrador's not reach, just in case someone leaves the door open by mistake.

Make sure there are no poisonous plants, such as euphorbia or monkshood, in the borders, and ensure that no poisonous cocoa mulch has been used anywhere. If there are any of these, remove them all and donate to dog-free friends. If you want a full list of plants that are poisonous to dogs, ask for advice at your local garden centre, or do some research on the internet.

If a fox has made its den under your garden shed or even under your neighbour's garden shed, contact the local council pest control department to remove and relocate the occupants; fox mange, which is prevalent in both the rural and urban fox, can easily pass to your dog.

PREPARATIONS INSIDE

CLEARING THE DECKS
In the house, you need to decide which rooms your dog will be allowed to occupy. Will he have free range of all the rooms, upstairs and downstairs, or will there be no-go areas?

A puppy is best kept in the kitchen/utility room until he is house trained, and he must not be allowed to climb up stairs until he is fully mature. An adult Labrador may be allowed more freedom. However, do remember that your Labrador's legs, paws and under-body will often get very wet and muddy during exercise. He will certainly need drying off and cleaning up with a towel before being allowed into the sitting room!

If you have rooms displaying

An inquisitive puppy will wreak havoc in your home if he is not properly supervised.

precious Dresden ornaments or priceless antique furniture, I suggest you class these as no-go areas. One swipe of a Labrador's happily wagging tail can easily cause an expensive disaster, and the odd nibble at the leg of an original Chippendale chair might well prove unpopular, too!

When you have selected the rooms where your Labrador is to be allowed, put all remaining valuable items up high, out of reach, especially spectacle cases and remote controls for TVs, DVD players and videos, which Labradors find delectably crunchy! Make sure there are no trailing electric cables in areas where he might be passing through.

Finally, Labradors have little conscience where food is concerned. Make sure the fridge, pantry door and kitchen cupboards are all firmly shut and your shopping bags are out of

reach. If your dog learns to open lever door-handles, which many Labs do if there is food on the other side, replace them with circular doorknobs! A fridge lock may come in useful, too.

AN INDOOR HOME
If you are bringing a puppy home, decide beforehand where you wish him to live as he grows up, and then you can locate his crate/indoor kennel (see page 55). A dog likes to live in the hub of the family, rather than being left in an isolated room, far away from all the daily goings-on. The ideal place is the kitchen or utility room, particularly if either room has quick access to the back door to aid initial toilet training.

Do not site the indoor kennel in a glass conservatory, unless it is well ventilated and fully shaded. In most cases, a conservatory will be too hot in summer (even with the windows open), and too cold in the winter.

If you are taking on an adult, locate the indoor kennel in the kitchen, utility or living room, so that your Labrador can be with you as much as possible.

GETTING THE GEAR

You can purchase most equipment – beds, bedding, crates, playpens, bowls, collars and leads – from your local pet store, pet supermarket, online, or by mail-order via the adverts in specialist dog newspapers and magazines.

- **Old newspapers:** In the preceding weeks, prior to your dog's arrival, collect a stack of old, clean newspapers, which will be invaluable when house training the puppy in its early days with you. If you are rehoming an adult Labrador, you will be prepared in case of a first-night 'accident'.

- **Dog beds:** These come in spectacular shapes and sizes, and it is tempting to buy a cosy bed for a new arrival. However, puppies often chew their beds, so it is better not to waste your money by buying an expensive bed at this stage. The best plan is to use a 24-inch (60-cm) plastic puppy bed, or a large cardboard box (making sure it has no metal staples). You can replace the cardboard box when it gets chewed up or squashed, and once the puppy is fully grown, you can buy him an easily cleaned, adult plastic dog bed. The minimum size for an adult Labrador is 27 inches by 18 inches (68 x 46 cm). There are expensive foam-filled dogs beds, available in every manner of shapes and sizes, but in all likelihood your Labrador will just chew the bed to dig out the foam. So, unless you are prepared to replace the bed frequently, you are better off choosing a durable, plastic bed.

The same applies to wicker dog beds. They look good, are deliciously chewable and last only a few minutes!

- **Bedding:** The best choice is synthetic bedding, which can be easily washed and dried. Ideally, you will need at least three pieces so that there is always bedding available. Dog bedding should be regularly washed in the washing machine with non-biological washing powder (biological powder can cause skin irritation). Synthetic bedding comes in a range of colours: brown or dark green are practical colours; white, blue and yellow look attractive, but soon show the dirt. For a puppy, you can use an old woollen blanket. The pup will doubtless shred the blanket as the days go by, but you can throw it away and replace it when it becomes tatty. Regardless of whether you have a puppy or an adult, it is not advisable to use padded bedding. When there is nothing exciting going on, a Labrador's joy is to quietly nibble open all the seams and slowly extract the wadding, bit by bit, which can prove dangerous if swallowed and makes a mess when spread all over the floor.

A Labrador grows so fast that you may decide to use a temporary bed, such as a cardboard box, to begin with.

A SAFE HAVEN

The best purchase you can make is a wire-mesh indoor dog kennel/crate, which will give your Labrador his own special home within your home. Most of the time you can leave the door open, so your dog can wander in and out as he pleases. The crate, which is easily dismantled, should have a removable, plastic tray in the base and be a minimum size of 24 inches by 37 inches, and 27 inches high (61 x 94 x 68 cm), which is suitable for an adult Labrador. Designs vary, but the kennel will have one or two opening doors.

An indoor kennel is invaluable when you are rearing a puppy, as you have a safe place to confine him at night. A puppy is also safer shut in the crate at times when he cannot be supervised, such as when you pop out for a short time to go to the local shops. The puppy cannot get into mischief while you are away if he is shut in, whereas if he is loose, he might opt to try out his new teeth on your kitchen cupboards. The crate will also become his sanctuary when non dog-loving relations come to visit, wearing expensive light-coloured clothes, or when hoards of excited, tail-pulling children descend to play.

Before you fetch your Labrador, set up the crate ready, in your chosen area. Cover the crate-tray in the base with plenty of newspaper. If you are rearing a puppy, put the cardboard box dog bed, or the plastic puppy bed, at the back of the kennel, lining it with newspaper and with bedding. If your new Labrador is an adult, place a piece of bedding on the plastic base tray.

IN THE HOUSE

You may want allocate the utility area or part of the kitchen as your 'doggy area' of the house.

A stairgate is a useful barrier to prevent a puppy going upstairs or straying into parts of the house where he cannot be properly supervised.

• **Puppy playpen:** As well as the crate, you may wish to buy a puppy playpen, if you have sufficient space. A playpen is made from several individual interlinked 3ft high (90 cm) wire-mesh panels and can be used indoors or outdoors. It can be easily dismantled and allows the puppy a secure, controlled play area. It will only be safe to use in the first four months, as a growing pup will quickly learn to climb out of it. However, a playpen is a useful, short-term training aid.

• **Stairgate:** If you do not want your Labrador to go upstairs, you can fit a stairgate at the foot of the stairs. Remember, a puppy must not be allowed climb stairs while he is growing, as this could damage his limbs. If you want to take your puppy upstairs, you will have to carry him both up and downstairs.

An adult Labrador will quickly learn how to open simple catches on stairgates, so choose one with a flip-over, locking catch, operated by depressing two safety buttons.

• **Feeding bowls and water buckets:** Dishes come in all shapes and sizes. Because your Labrador is likely to pick up his bowl and wander around with it in his mouth, unbreakable, stainless steel bowls are best; fancy pottery bowls do not survive long when dropped on the tiled kitchen floor! You will need at least three stainless steel feeding bowls. The best size is 8 to 10 inches (20 to 25.5 cm), preferably with cone-shaped sides and a non-slip bottom rim (a bit like a dunce's hat with the top half inverted). Because of the conical shape, a Labrador is unlikely to pick up the bowl.

A stainless steel water pail, which can be sited outdoors during the day (except in frosty weather), is also a good idea. Bring the water bucket in at night, as rats, which can carry a nasty disease that is transmittable to dogs, can visit even the cleanest of outdoor places at night.

All dishes and buckets should be washed daily in warm soapy water and rinsed well.

• **Collar and lead:** An eight-week-old puppy will not be lead trained; however, when you go to collect him, take a 15-inch (38-cm) soft-nylon puppy collar and a non-leather lead, just in case you have an emergency, such as the car breaking down on the journey home. Do not buy an expensive leather lead at this stage, as your puppy will probably chew it. The first collar you buy will be outgrown very quickly, so you will need to replace it with a second collar, which can be adjusted as the puppy gets bigger. Do not leave a collar on a youngster when he is running free, unsupervised, in your garden. If a sturdy branch of a shrub gets caught through the collar, it could end in tragedy.

For an adult dog, the best choice is a rounded leather collar or a plain nylon collar, around 24-26 inches (61-66 cm) long. I prefer a leather lead, as nylon leads can cut your hands if the dog pulls unexpectedly.

Extending/retractable leads are also very useful, as you can give your dog controlled exercise in areas where dogs are not allowed off the lead.

• **Grooming kit:** When your puppy first arrives in his new home, he will not need much coat care, but he needs to get used to the routine of being brushed. Initially, you can buy a soft brush, and spend a few minutes each day grooming your puppy so that he gets used to being handled. It is also important to practise opening your puppy's mouth, and then giving him a treat, so that he accepts teeth cleaning. (For information on grooming the adult Labrador, see Chapter 5: The Best of Care.)

• **Toys:** Labradors of all ages love playing with squeaky toys, rubber rings, plastic dumbbells, rope tugs, and even empty plastic bottles (with the screw top removed). Soft toys are available in plenty from local charity shops. Make sure the toys are safe for very young children – which will suit also your dog – as there will be no removable parts, which could be detached and swallowed.

For a puppy, try a Nylabone ring or bone, which is a virtually indestructible, chewable toy for teething, or a squeaky, prickly, plastic hedgehog. For an adult, buy a rubber Kong, which, when thrown, bounces in erratic directions, providing lots of fun. It can also be filled with food!

Adult Labradors love to play for hours on end and will happily retrieve anything you care to throw. Old tennis balls are ideal, but never throw sticks or stones.

Check that toys are 100 per cent safe before giving them to your puppy.

At last, the day comes when it is time to collect your puppy.

COLLECTING YOUR LABRADOR

If you are travelling by car to collect your new Labrador, consider how you will look after the puppy or adult during the journey home. If there is no one to accompany you, put a crate in the car for the puppy to travel in, or fit a dog guard to keep an adult safely in the rear of the vehicle. A puppy must not be loose during the journey, as this could be very dangerous.

Be prepared for doggy accidents en-route, drooling or car sickness etc, and take a roll of kitchen towels, an old terry towel, a blanket, some newspaper, and a black rubbish bag. Remember, to bring the collar and lead you purchased earlier, and also pack a water bowl, a bottle of drinking water, and some Biscrok or similar biscuits, in case the journey is prolonged for any reason.

When you are ready to collect your puppy, arrange to arrive in the morning, so your Labrador has plenty of time to settle in his new home before nightfall. If you are purchasing a puppy, you will probably have already visited the breeder and had a peep at your puppy when he was about five weeks old. Hopefully, the breeder will have given you a detailed list of the things you should assemble prior to the puppy's collection. When you pick up the puppy, you will be given a copy of his Kennel Club registration certificate and a copy of his four- or five-generation pedigree, with details of the sire, starting at the top left-hand side of the page, and of the dam, lower down the left-hand side. The pedigree will show the puppy's relations, with Champions printed in red.

HEALTH CERTIFICATES

The puppy's parents should both have a Kennel Club/British Veterinary Association KC/BVA hip score (the current breed average score is 15-16 but the lower the score, the better). In the USA, a similar scheme is operated by the Orthopaedic Foundation for Animals (OFA); X-rays are evaluated using a seven-point scoring system. The parents should both have a clear annual eye test certificate (for more information on inherited disorders, see Chapter 8: Happy and Healthy). You will be given copies of these certificates, plus insurance for the first six weeks of ownership, which will cover any unexpected vet bills or loss of your puppy. As youngsters are extremely mischievous, accidents can happen, and, ideally, the puppy insurance should be continued for at least the first 12 months of his life, which is the main age when injuries occur.

REARING STRATEGY

The breeder will want to spend time going through detailed rearing instructions with you. This will include information on the puppy's diet, and the worming treatment he has received. All puppies are born with roundworms and the breeder will have wormed him at regular 14-day intervals up to the time you collect him. The breeder will also advise on how much exercise the puppy should be allowed, lead training, and house training. The breeder will have reared the puppy since birth with great care and attention, and will emphasise that it is your responsibility to continue the process.

CONTRACT OF SALE

In most cases, you will be asked to read and sign a Contract of Sale. This is a legal document, which confirms that you have received and understood all the paperwork the breeder has given you, including copies of the health checks, the registration documents, and the rearing instructions. It may also include an agreement that should you ever need to rehome the dog, you will do so through the proper channels, most likely by contacting the breeder in the first instance, who will probably take the dog back.

FEEDING INSTRUCTIONS

FOOD FOR PUPPIES

In the past, puppies were fed meat, wholemeal biscuit and additives. These days, most Labrador puppies are fed all-in-one, balanced, dried food specifically made for puppies. The breeder will give you a few days' supply of the particular food the puppy has been weaned on and a diet sheet stating how much to feed.

Initially, at eight weeks of age, the puppy will have four regularly spaced meals daily, at approximately 7.30am, 12 noon, 5pm and 9pm, increasing in amount, but decreasing in number to one or two meals a day by the time the dog is 12 months of age. Guidelines on the amount to feed are set out in grams on the side of the product bag. Weigh the food; do not guess. It is important that no additional supplements are added to all-in-one balanced food, as this could cause bone-growth abnormalities. Because the food is dry, plentiful drinking water must be available day and night.

It is inadvisable to change the diet or substitute other brands of food until the puppy has settled in, otherwise his tummy may become upset. If you do change the food for whatever reason, take several days to do so, gradually mixing the new food in with the old food. Use your eyes to keep a constant check on your puppy's weight. At this rapid growing stage, he needs to be well covered, not gross, but more importantly not slim. If you have any concerns over your puppy's weight, ask your vet for advice.

The breeder will give you detailed information on how the puppies have been reared.

Do not make any changes to your puppy's diet when he first arrives home.

BANNED FOOD

- Never give your Labrador large, bone-shaped hide chews from the pet shop; many Labradors have died swallowing these whole. Sadly, once in the gut, they absorb moisture, expand, and cause a complete blockage, which the vet usually finds impossible to remove.
- Do not feed cows' milk; older puppies and adult Labradors cannot digest the lactose.
- Do not feed chocolate intended for human use, which contains theobromine, a substance highly poisonous to dogs. It only takes 200 grams of dark chocolate to kill a Labrador.
- For the same reason, do not use cocoa mulch in the garden, as it also contains theobromine.
- Onions and grapes/raisins are also toxic to dogs.

For more information on feeding your Labrador, See Chapter 5: The Best of Care.

FOOD FOR ADULTS

The breeder or rescue charity will give you details of the food your adult Lab is used to. He may have one or two meals daily, plus a Bonio-type biscuit for breakfast and at bedtime. As with a puppy, any changes to his diet must be carried out over several days.

If you wish to give your Labrador a bone, make sure it is a large, fresh marrowbone. Cooked marrow bones tend to splinter badly, so raw ones are better. Scrape most of the very rich marrow fat out with a spoon and give the bone for around half an hour. If your Labrador has the bone for longer, he will grind the whole thing up, swallow it all and make himself sick.

EXERCISE

Labrador puppies are full of energy and fun, but they must not be over-exercised in their first year. Their growing bones do not calcify until they are fully mature. It has been found that the age at which calcification/final hardening of the leg bones is completed, with all growth plates closed, is influenced by coat colour. In yellow Labradors, calcification occurs at around 12 months; in black and chocolate Labradors, it occurs at 16 to 18 months. Once the bones have fully calcified, exercise may be given freely. However, if the puppy is over exercised before this time, permanent damage could be done to the skeletal frame, possibly damaging hips, hocks or elbows, which might be the cause of arthritis in later life.

It is essential to monitor exercise when a Labrador puppy is growing.

Before vaccinations are completed (see page 131), the puppy cannot go out unless he is carried. It is advisable to avoid contact with dogs outside the home. In the period up to six months of age, a puppy needs very little exercise, apart from a run around your well-fenced garden. It is important to take him in the car to socialise him at shops and outside schools (see Chapter 6: Socialisation and Training), but he should not be allowed long walks. Do not be tempted to throw things too far

for small puppies to retrieve; their exercise should be very gentle with no violent galloping or turning.

From six to 12 months of age, you can allow your Labrador an increasing amount of exercise on the lead, aiming for two miles daily by the time he is 12 months. From 12 to 18 months, the exercise can be increased until you can take him wherever you wish to go for the rest of his life.

If your Labrador goes swimming in cold water, make

sure his lower back and the root of his tail is properly dried, otherwise he may get 'dead tail' where the tail hangs limply for several days. It is similar to neuralgia in humans, and is very painful for the dog. It takes about 10 days to clear (see Chapter 8: Happy and Healthy).

Throwing sticks should always be avoided, as a Labrador – puppy or adult – could damage the inside of his mouth and throat very badly. Likewise, do not throw stones for your dog to retrieve; they could break his teeth. The safest article to retrieve is a tennis ball. Labradors adore chasing footballs, but it is not a good idea, as a dog can end up with badly injured toes and needing veterinary treatment, such is their forceful enthusiasm for the game!

FINDING A VET

The first step is to ask other dog owners in your area which vet they use. Addresses can also be found in the Yellow Pages or local business directories. Make an appointment to see the vet within a couple of days of collecting your Lab. He can then carry out a full health check-up. If you have a puppy and he is around 8 to 10 weeks of age, the vet will commence the puppy's vaccinations; the second

vaccination is given two weeks later (see page 131).

The vet will want to know when the dog was last wormed and will probably provide further worming tablets. Do not worm a puppy on the same day as he is vaccinated. This can quite often make him poorly. Wait at least three days after his vaccination before worming. The vet will also advise on regular flea and tick treatment for your new puppy or adult (see Chapter 8: Happy and Healthy).

If you want your puppy microchipped, this is usually done at the time of the second vaccination. The chip resembles a small grain of rice and is painlessly inserted in the scruff of the neck. It contains the dog's individual identification number,

which will appear on a national register with your address. This is invaluable if your dog is ever lost.

MEETING THE FAMILY

Whether you have decided to rehome an adult, or take on a puppy, do not overwhelm him with too many visitors as soon as you arrive home. First of all, offer your Labrador a drink of water, then take him to his toilet spot in the garden. An adult Lab can be taken on the lead, and then given a chance to get his bearings and settle in gradually.

A puppy can be loose while he is being shown the kitchen and the garden. Let him meet the children; they will be very excited, but they should try to be calm so as not to frighten him.

Arrange for a health check within a couple of days of collecting your puppy to ensure he is fit and well.

To start with, you must supervise all interactions with children.

Allow the children to pat and stroke the puppy gently. Never allow youngsters to pick up a puppy; he will be too heavy and wriggly, and could go crashing to the floor. A puppy should be held on a parent's lap for the children to stroke.

Always let the children play with the pup while they are sitting on the floor and not standing up. Make them aware that the puppy has very sharp teeth and scratchy claws and to keep their faces away from the puppy. Do not let them or their friends torment the puppy by holding him down and tickling his feet, or pulling his ears or tail. If things get too exuberant, put the puppy in his crate for a while with a treat.

If the puppy or adult is shy, do not over-face him; leave him be

for the time being. After a while, offer your dog his first dinner. Food is the way to a Labrador's heart. He will probably forget his apprehension, gobble his dinner and from then on be completely won over by your family forever.

DOG TO DOG

If you have another dog in the family, it is better for them to meet outside in the garden. If the new arrival is an adult, keep him on the lead and make a great fuss of the resident dog as you introduce the newcomer. Remember not to make the existing pet jealous. He should get most of the love and attention, and a few extra treats. If you are introducing a puppy to an older dog, do not allow the older dog to assert himself roughly. The first introduction

should be carried out with the puppy in a crate, so the two dogs get to know each other through the wire mesh. If you sense antagonism from the older dog, such as growling, you may be advised to continue supervised meetings, with the puppy in the crate, until the adult has accepted the newcomer. I advise people to wait a couple of days before allowing the two to meet 'in the open'. The next step is to sit with the puppy on your lap, and let the two dogs sniff each other. Give them both lots of praise, and when you judge all is well, put the pup on the floor. If you take time over the initial introductions, all should go well. Do not let a puppy make free with the other dog's toys, bed or food, and never leave the puppy with an older dog at this

63

If relationships start on a good footing, a Labrador and a cat will live peaceably together.

introductory stage.

It is also important not to allow a puppy to run freely with an adult dog for some months. Play sessions tend to get too rough, and some adults delight in running puppies down. This could cause permanent damage to growing bones.

DOG TO CAT

A cat may be very aloof when a new dog comes to join the family or she may be scared witless, depending on her personality and past experiences. As long as a cat can keep her dignity, escape out of the way without being chased, ensure her bed is not taken up and her dinner is not gobbled up, she may become good friends with her canine companion. It is a good idea to install a stairgate, so that the cat can rest upstairs undisturbed and escape the new dog's attentions if she wants to.

Remember, a puppy is likely to come off worse with any argument with the family cat. Eyes can be badly damaged, so extra vigilance is needed.

THE FIRST NIGHT

Many new owners dread the first night, fearing the puppy will be distressed and cry all night. However, with careful management, this does not have to be the case. After the puppy has met everyone, eaten, played and toileted outside, he should then go to bed in his indoor kennel with a biscuit. He may be so tired after the experiences of such a busy day that he just drops off to sleep all night, until you wake him for outside toileting at breakfast-time the following morning.

Alternatively, he may howl plaintively for a few hours and feel utterly dejected, lonely and chilly; being on his own for the very first time without his brothers and sisters to keep him snug. It is very difficult to harden your heart and ignore his cries. Ideally you should do this, but most owners will end up leaving their bed upstairs to go down to comfort the sad little fellow, who, in turn, thinks, "Wow, this is great: if I want to see my owner in the middle of the night, all I've got to do is howl a bit more!" In the end, he will settle.

A radio turned on low or a loud ticking alarm-clock will help to make a puppy feel he is not completely alone, and a hot-water bottle or heated pad under his blanket in his bed will also make him more relaxed. Do not be tempted to take him to your bed – you could roll on him and squash him! If you can't bear the sound of his cries, for this first night only, take his indoor kennel upstairs and set it up beside your bed. Carry the puppy upstairs and put him in the kennel. He should sleep soundly then, but the next night you really will have to make him sleep downstairs.

BEING SAFE

When you initially take your puppy home, you will find that he will need lots of food and sleep in his first few months, interspersed with gentle playtime and plenty of love. There are some other guidelines to bear in mind during this period:

• Labrador puppies are very lively. You must be the one to dictate the manner of play, otherwise he will simply career around to the point of exhaustion.

• Before vaccinations are complete, do not let adult dogs from other households meet your puppy. When attending the surgery for his vaccinations wait in the car, or keep your puppy on your lap when you are waiting in the reception area. Never put your puppy on the floor where poorly dogs may have been.

• Do not let your puppy jump in and out of your car, climb up and down stairs or climb steep door steps. He must not jump on and off furniture, or slide about on tiled floors.

• If the puppy has been sitting on your lap, when you stand up, hold him tightly to put him on the ground and make sure all his four feet are in contact with the floor before you release him and stand up.

• In this growing period all games must be gentle; sudden twisting and turning is not

Your puppy is bound to feel bewildered the first night in his new home.

good for the puppy's growing frame.

• If there are times when you cannot supervise your puppy, leave him in his indoor kennel where he can come to no harm.

HOUSE TRAINING

A Labrador puppy that has been well reared by his breeder will be used to using newspaper in his toilet area. Once he comes to live with you, the newspaper should

be spread by the back door. As he gets used to using the paper, open the back door and move the paper outside.

As soon as a puppy wakes, after he has eaten, and after play sessions, a puppy will want to relieve himself. He should be taken outside to the spot in the garden you have chosen for him to use. When he goes, give him lots of praise and he will very soon get the message. You can introduce a verbal command,

It is important to stick to a routine when you are house training a puppy.

such as "Busy" or "Hurry up", and, in time, your pup will learn to associate the command with the appropriate action.

There are bound to be accidents. If you witness the accident, say "No!" with a stern voice and encourage him outside. If you are not there when he has an accident, do not scold him when you finally do see what has happened. He will not remember what he has done and will not understand why his lovely owner is so cross.

If the puppy gets excited, he will also want to relieve himself: watch out for your pup darting around rapidly in circles and possibly squeaking, usually after a period of play. This is a sure sign he wants to go outside, in which case, scoop him up and take him outside to the toilet spot. Praise any results lavishly.

It will only take a few days to house train your puppy if you are vigilant at all times. At night, the pup will sleep in his bed in his crate with the door shut. His water bowl will be in the crate with him. Dogs and puppies do

not like to foul their crates and this makes it easy to house train them quickly.

WEARING A COLLAR AND LEAD

Your puppy can get used to wearing his collar and lead in the house and in the garden. First, put on the collar and distract his attention so he does not worry about it. It may be a few days before a puppy gets used to his collar and stops scratching at it. Remember not to leave the collar on when the

DOGS IN CARS

You will need to purchase a suitable dog guard or a dog crate to fit your car. Do not take the dog in the car if there is any chance you will have to leave it parked in sunshine – even for a few minutes. It is possible for the temperature within a car to rise so rapidly that the dog's internal organs literally cook and the dog could die.

If you are going on a long journey, fit blinds to the rear window; the dog should not be subjected to scorching sunshine for miles on end. Ensure enough air is circulated in the back of the car and preferably travel with the air conditioning on. Take plenty of water and a water bowl with you.

A treat will encourage your puppy to move forward on the lead. Use the pup's name to attract his attention, and then look ahead as you move off.

puppy is unsupervised in case of accidents. Once the puppy is used to the collar, attach the lead and gently walk forward, looking ahead, not at the puppy. Give lots of verbal encouragement. He will soon follow you. Do not let him pull, but keep him by your side. (For more training information, see Chapter 6.)

HOUSE RULES

A Labrador puppy's brain is initially like a blank canvas. He has to find out what is acceptable and what is not, by trying everything out. You are the one to teach him and establish the house rules; if you say "No", then he knows that he is doing something he should not do. If you praise him, then he concludes his actions must be correct. You should establish no-go areas, and teach him good manners: no begging for food at the table, no shoe chewing, no stealing, no digging up the lawn and no stone eating. Ideally, when he is old enough, take him to a Good Citizen training class (see Chapter 6: Socialisation and Training) where he will learn to become a thoroughly well-mannered dog of whom you can be justifiably proud for many years to come.

THE BEST OF CARE

Chapter 5

Labrador Retrievers are generally healthy dogs due to their medium size and lack of exaggerated features. However, there are particular characteristics of the breed, such as a tendency to do well on even comparatively small amounts of food, which can lead to problems, such as obesity. Conscientious breeders do their utmost to reduce the incidence of inherited diseases, such as hip or elbow dysplasia, by using approved veterinary schemes as a guide to selecting suitable breeding stock. But these diseases are only partially caused by the Labrador's genetic make-up. Environmental factors, such as diet and exercise, also contribute to the development of these and similar conditions. Over-exercising puppies and young Labradors causes strain or damage on growing bones and joints, while insufficient regular exercise in the

adult Labrador will deny him sufficient opportunity to build up the right amount of protective muscle and strength. Such management failures will exacerbate or even create health problems in what would otherwise have been a fit and healthy dog.

Generally, once adult, the Labrador is an easygoing, good-natured dog. However, in a breed originally developed to serve man as an intelligent working gundog, insufficient mental stimulation of the correct sort, and particularly during the first few years, can lead to boredom and the subsequent development of behavioural and training problems. Providing the Labrador owner recognises these potential pitfalls, takes sensible, knowledgeable advice and uses common sense, a trouble-free, happy life with your Labrador is the most likely outcome. In this chapter I will describe the dietary, physical and mental exercise

requirements for your Labrador, covering the different life stages from puppy through to adolescent, adult and veteran, and I will address the treatment of some common ailments.

DIET AND NUTRITION

In order to understand the differing needs of your Labrador from puppyhood to veteran, it is necessary to explain a little about the nutrients that make up the diet. This is important because either too little or too many of the correct nutrients, vitamins and minerals can cause problems or disease. Also, there are so many commercial diets on the market, and so many opinions expressed, that a basic understanding of the subject can help the owner to make informed choices on their dog's diet.

WATER
Water is essential for all life, and the dog's body usually consists of

between 60 and 80 per cent water. Young dogs having a higher content, while adults have a higher fat content. Without water, the dog will die in a few days. The dog's normal daily water requirement in millilitres is approximately equal to his daily energy requirement in kilocalories. Fresh water should always be available.

UNDERSTANDING PROTEIN

There are many different types of protein; some are suitable for the diet and some are not. The waste products from protein digestion are converted in the dog's liver and then excreted by the kidneys. Proteins are made up of chains of smaller components called amino acids. The dog requires 10 different types of these amino acids in the diet. These are called essential amino acids, as they either cannot be made within the dog's body from other sources, or not at a rate

WHY DOGS NEED PROTEIN

Growth and repair of body tissues and organs, including the skin, provides strength and flexibility in muscles, tendons and cartilage and aids the formation of lubricants. It forms some essential components of the blood, immunity and hormone (endocrine) systems. Proteins are also needed for the transportation of some other nutrients around the body.

that is quick enough to meet the dog's daily requirements. The most suitable dietary proteins are those that are made up of amino acids that most closely match the dog's daily essential amino acid requirement. Where there is a close amino acid match, called a

high biological value (HBV) protein, the dog will need less of this food to meet his daily requirements. Also, the waste products of protein digestion are kept to a minimum, which tends to reduce the amount of work required of the liver and kidneys. HBV proteins are usually more expensive to feed: for example, cooked eggs, fish-meal, and some meats. In contrast, lower biological value proteins, such as wheat, corn or soybean, are more economical to buy. It is worth noting that although milk is a HBV food, adult dogs usually lack the enzyme necessary to digest it.

UNDERSTANDING FATS AND OILS

Fats are made up of chains of fatty acids and other components. They are sometimes referred to as lipids. There are two main types of dietary fat:
• **Saturated fats:** which contain

The amount of water that a dog requires depends on his daily energy requirements.

WHY DOGS NEED FAT

Fat is a major source of energy and weight, for fat produces twice the calories of protein or carbohydrates. It helps the body absorb and transport certain vitamins; it is essential in the manufacture of some hormones and therefore for reproduction and pregnancy. It helps form the cell walls, provides insulation and maintains skin health. Through sebum secretion, it protects the coat hairs and waterproofs them.

A Labrador grows very rapidly in the first few months of life, and protein is therefore an essential part of the diet.

cholesterol, which is needed to support and repair the walls of body cells.

• **Unsaturated fats:** which contain three types of essential fatty acids that are needed by the dog. One of these – linoleic acid or omega 6 – can be used to make a certain amount of the other two – linolenic acid or omega 3, and arachidonic acid, which is only found in animal fats and is also an omega 6.

Fats that solidify at room temperature, such as lard and butter, are lower in unsaturated fatty acids; those that are liquid at room temperature, such as corn oil or linseed oil, are higher in unsaturated fatty acids. Fish oil is particularly rich in omega 3 and recent research suggests it is beneficial when appropriately added to a dog's diet. The appropriate ratio of one fat type to another is as important as the total amount of fat in a diet to keep your dog healthy.

UNDERSTANDING CARBOHYDRATES

Carbohydrates are not an essential nutrient for dogs. However, they are useful in the diet, as once certain types of soluble carbohydrates (such as alpha monosaccharides or polysaccharides/starch) are broken down during digestion, they become glucose and are readily absorbed and used as energy. Although the breakdown products of protein and fats are also stored as glucose, the provision of carbohydrates is a more economical way of obtaining glucose.

Another type of carbohydrate – the beta monosaccharides or polysaccharides, such as cellulose – are not easily absorbed, as the dog does not have the necessary digestive microbes in the gut in the same quantity that herbaceous animals, such as cows, do. However, in appropriate amounts they can help with the action and health of the gut, and will produce a softer, bulkier stool that is easier to pass. In addition, they are useful in special diets for obese dogs by reducing the absorption of other nutrients while still filling the dog's stomach and making him feel full. Carbohydrates are contained in cereals, potatoes and rice.

UNDERSTANDING VITAMINS AND MINERALS

Vitamins are complex organic compounds. They are not nutrients in themselves, but they are necessary to ensure that the nutrients explained above can be digested and used by the body. There are 13 major vitamins contained in a wide variety of foods. Some are absorbed from the gut, along with fat (fat-soluble), and can be stored in the body. These are vitamins A, D, E and K. The B complex vitamins (eight vitamins) and vitamin C are water-soluble. They are not stored in the body in significant amounts, so a daily intake is required. They are excreted in the urine, so deficiencies may result during excessive water loss, such as diarrhoea. Some vitamins are produced in the animal's body. For example, vitamin K is produced by intestinal bacteria.

The processing and storage of food decreases its active vitamin content. However, pet food manufacturers compensate for this by adding vitamins to their products.

Minerals are inorganic substances that form less than one per cent of bodyweight, but they are essential for correct growth and the functioning of the body. They also form complex reactions among themselves, meaning excesses or imbalances may have a knock-on effect on other minerals. They include macrominerals (e.g. calcium, phosphorus and sodium) that are required in one part per hundred in the diet, i.e. 10 grams per kilogram of diet, and microminerals (such as selenium, iodine and zinc) that are required in one part per million, i.e. one milligram per kilogram of diet.

CHOOSING A DIET

Your puppy should have come with a diet sheet provided by his breeder. As long as this is a sensible diet, which is balanced to suit the puppy's nutritional needs (ask your vet for confirmation),

If your Labrador is thriving, there is no need to change his diet.

Nutritional requirements depend on your dog's lifestyle.

and is readily available, there will be no necessity to change it. Obviously, you will need to make appropriate modifications as the puppy grows (see below).

READING FOOD LABELS
There are a number of legal requirements that manufacturers have to follow when labelling dog food. A quick look at any proprietary food will show what they are. Labelling must include a typical analysis of the food based on the whole contents of a tin or packet including water. As foods have different water contents, in order to make a more accurate comparison of ingredients the percentage of each ingredient needs to be obtained using a dry-weight basis. Therefore, if you wish to compare the protein content of a tin (which normally has 80 per cent moisture) and a dry food (which normally has 20

per cent moisture), both having 10 per cent protein, the following calculation is needed:

- The tin with 80 per cent moisture has 100 - 80 = 20 per cent dry matter.
- Calculate the protein in the tin as 10 per cent of 20 per cent dry matter.
- Therefore 10 divided by 20 x 100 = 50 per cent protein.

- The dry food with 20 per cent moisture has 100 - 20 = 80 per cent dry matter.
- Calculate the protein in the dry food as 10 per cent of 80 per cent dry matter.
- Therefore 10 divided by 80 x 100 = 12.5 per cent of protein

In this calculation you can see that the tin actually has four times as much protein as the dry food. The same calculations can be used

for the other nutrients involved.

FEEDING FOR LIFE STAGES
If we look at requirements for the various life stages in simple terms, we will see that puppies need higher protein and fat levels than adult dogs in order to grow properly. They also have smaller stomachs, so they need good-quality protein and low-bulk foods. Dogs of seven and over are entering their older age and should not consume high amounts of protein, as the excretion of its waste products puts extra strain on the kidneys, which tend to wear out in old age. It is best if older dogs get their energy requirements from higher levels of fat and/or carbohydrate. Working dogs benefit from higher levels of fat, as this reduces the bulk of the feed for the same amount of calories. Dogs find it difficult to work on a full or over-extended stomach.

TYPES OF FOOD

TYPE OF FOOD	ADVANTAGES	DISADVANTAGES
HOME-MADE DIET Owner selects ingredients and mixes own diet. Ingredients used might be cooked or raw. 	• Full knowledge by owner of ingredients used to make the diet. • Can adjust diet to suit animal preferences or sensitivities. • Opportunity to use only fresh ingredients. • Where the appropriate ingredients are used, it can be a very natural way of feeding, being close to the diet eaten by the wild dog.	• Owner needs to have a very good understanding of nutrition to ensure the diet is balanced for a dog's nutritional needs. • Diet will need changing and adjusting over the animal's life to suit different life stages. • Might not always be possible to obtain the normally used ingredients. • Non-cooked foods may have a higher risk of carrying infectious organisms or parasites and go off quicker. • Cooking can destroy or reduce some nutrients. • Time-consuming.
PROPRIETARY FOODS Manufactured especially for dogs and may be moist, semi-moist or dry foods. Classified into two categories: **complementary foods** and **complete foods** (see page 75).	• Convenient to feed. • Wide range of products in a wide price range. • Moist and semi-moist foods are usually highly palatable for the dog and tend to be more digestible than dried foods. • Variety of ways to produce a balanced diet. • Their look and smell often appeal to owners.	• High palatability can lead to over eating and obesity. • Correct storage arrangements are needed for moist or opened foods that can easily go off or dry out.

TYPE OF FOOD

COMPLEMENTARY FOODS
Fed on their own they are not nutritionally balanced but are designed to be added to other ingredients to ensure this.

Examples include:
- Wholemeal biscuit, which must be added to fresh, frozen, canned or other processed meat or protein source.
- Dried meats and most canned meats designed to be fed with wholemeal biscuit or other cereal-based products.
- Treats.

COMPLETE FOODS
Provide a complete, balanced and adequate diet when fed on their own.
Examples include:
- All-in-one dried foods and some canned or heat-sealed foods.
- Dry complete foods are produced either in an extruded kibble form or a loose mix.

ADVANTAGES

- Easy for owners to feed.
- Some canned moist complete foods are especially useful for sensitive digestive systems as are some of the most expensive complete foods, which usually have a fixed formula with the same raw ingredients in the same quantities used for each batch, providing consistency.
- Dried foods rely on their low moisture content to prevent them going off and are comparatively easy to store.
- Kibble, when fed dry, may help prevent plaque or tartar formation on the teeth. However, palatability may be increased by the addition of water.
- A wide range of specialist diets to suit all life stages and some medical conditions are available, e.g. obesity diets and diets on veterinary prescription. Some diets are manufactured especially for the Labrador, taking account of their breed predispositions, e.g. tendency to obesity, arthritis and necessity for greater oil content in the coat.

DISADVANTAGES

- Especially in cheaper foods, the raw ingredients may vary or be in different quantities within each batch manufactured. These subtle changes may cause digestive upsets in dogs with sensitive digestive systems. Dried foods are sometimes less palatable.
- Dogs or owners may get bored with the same daily diet.
- Owners are often tempted to add their own additional ingredients, therefore making the diet unbalanced.
- Feeding dry food without mixing it with water can make dogs more thirsty.
- Loose mixes or muesli-type mixes are often cheaper but less digestible. The dog will require more food to ensure adequate nutrition, providing more work for the digestive system and more faeces for the owner to clear up.

The following typical analysis below was taken from a range of dry foods manufactured for different lifestyles and stages and help to illustrate the point. There are also different needs for vitamins and minerals, but space does not permit more explanation here.

DIET Typical analysis	PROTEIN	FAT	FIBRE (carbohydrates)	ASH (minerals)
ADULT	20%	9%	4%	8.5%
PUPPY	29%	15%	2.5%	7.5%
SENIOR	18%	8.5%	4.5%	6%
WORKING	20%	10%	2.5%	6%

Appropriate calculations required to turn figures to % of dry matter. Assume 20 per cent moisture.

Below is an example diet for a puppy for the first year of life. The number of daily meals decreases over the weeks, but the amount fed at each meal increases as the puppy's stomach enlarges and is able to take more food. Any diet can only be used as a guide; owners need to use their eyes and hands to assess whether the puppy is too thin or too fat, and adjust the quantity to suit individual requirements. Some puppies, like people, need less food; some need more to maintain the same bodyweight. The simple body condition scoring chart (right) can also be used as a guide to help owners to assess this.

FEEDING REGIME

8 WEEKS TO 12 WEEKS
Four meals per day.

Breakfast and tea (meat-based meals)
4 to 5oz (113-142g) of meat with 2oz (56g) of puppy biscuit at each meal.

Initially, a puppy will need four meals a day.

Lunch and supper (milk-based meals)

$1/2$ pint of Lactol milk (a dried milk substitute for bitch's milk) (1oz (28g) of powder to $1/4$ pint (142ml) of water) with two cereal wheat biscuits at each meal OR, as an alternative, approximately 4 to 6oz (113-170g) or $1/4$ to $1/3$ of a large tin of rice pudding.

12 WEEKS TO 16 WEEKS
Three meals per day.

Breakfast and tea (meat-based meals)

$1/2$lb (227g) of meat with 4oz (113g) of puppy biscuit at each meal.

Lunch (milk-based meal)

$3/4$ pint (426ml) of Lactol ($1^1/2$ oz/42g of Lactol and 6fl.oz/170ml water) and three or four cereal wheat biscuits OR half a large can of rice pudding.

16 WEEKS TO 9 MONTHS
Two meals per day (meat-based meals).

1lb (453g) meat and $1/2$lb (227g) of biscuit at each meal.

NINE MONTHS ONWARDS
One meal per day (meat-based meal).

$1^1/2$ to 2lb (680-907g) of meat with 1lb (453g) of biscuit.

You may elect to split the daily food quantity into two meals, one in the morning and one in the evening. This will avoid overloading your Labrador Retriever's stomach.

BODY CONDITION SCORING CHART

EMACIATED
Obvious loss of muscle, no fat cover, ribs and pelvic bones easily seen.

THIN
Waist and abdominal tuck-up very clearly present, ribs seen, pelvic bones have very little cover.

IDEAL
Waist visible especially when seen from above, slight abdominal tuck-up, ribs can be felt but not seen.

OVERWEIGHT
Waist absent, abdominal tuck-up disappearing, ribs felt with difficulty, fat pads starting to form at base of tail on the back of the dog.

OBESE
Bulges in place of waist and abdominal tuck-up, ribs no longer can be felt, thick fat deposits at the base of the tail and on the shoulders.

Adult Labradors may be fed once a day, or the ration can be divided into two meals.

ROUTINE MANAGEMENT

I am a great believer in using a crate for day-to-day management in the first six months or so. Obviously, leaving the pup alone in the crate for a long period of time would be an abuse, and, apart from overnight, he should never be left for more than four hours. Most dogs end up loving their crates, and my older dogs will get inside one if they can, even though they have long since ceased needing to be confined. However, they were quickly conditioned to having a place to settle in, and the young Labrador's reputation for being a chewer can be redirected on to safe items.

EXERCISE

As we have learned in an earlier chapter, puppies do not need lots of walking during the first six months of life. But you will need to get your Labrador out and about so that he becomes properly socialised. You can only do this with practice, not just putting the dog in tempting situations and finding him wanting. (For further details on socialising your Labrador Retriever, see information in Chapter 6.)

When your Labrador has reached adulthood, he will need regular daily exercise. This should include some lead walking and some free-running exercise. If you are short of time, take a ball to the park, and you can play retrieve games, which will provide your Labrador with mental stimulation as well as physical exercise.

Labradors love to swim, and this is also great exercise for them. However, make sure that the conditions are safe for swimming, and check that there is an easy way for your Labrador Retriever to get out of the water before allowing him to take the plunge.

Remember, a fit dog is a happy and healthy dog, and your adult Labrador will thrive on as much exercise as you can manage to give him.

A Labrador that is fed a well-balanced diet and given regular exercise will avoid the dangers of obesity.

EXERCISING LABRADORS

Labradors cannot resist the water – and swimming is an excellent form of exercise.

If your puppy is handled from an early age, he will get used to the attention.

The next step is to brush him gently.

GROOMING LABRADORS

GROOMING

The Labrador is an easy dog to groom. He has a thick double coat: a waterproof topcoat, which repels dirt, and a warm, thick undercoat. To keep your dog clean, healthy and well groomed, you will need to give him a daily brush with a stiff dandy brush, which will remove dried mud. Do not try to brush mud off the coat until it is dry. After brushing, work through the coat with a wide-toothed comb, followed by a narrow-toothed comb to remove dead hairs. It is worth buying a dog towel, or collecting some old towels, which you can use for drying your Labrador after muddy or wet walks. If you want your dog's coat to gleam, buy a wash-leather and give him a rub down after grooming.

NAILS

The shape of a Labrador's foot means that as he walks on hard road surfaces, his nails will wear level and should not need trimming. However, if he is only exercised on grass, or if he has long toes, you may need to trim his nails every few weeks. The guillotine-type nail clippers are easiest to use. The nail is threaded through a hole in the clipper and is held steady while the cutting blade passes over the end of the nail, removing the excess. Ask someone to steady the dog's head while you trim the nails, and make sure you cut only the colourless part of the nail. Make sure you do not cut into the quick, which is the pink part of the claw, as it will bleed profusely. It is also painful for Labrador, so the next time he spies you with

the nail clippers, he will probably run and hide. You may also need to trim the dewclaws (the dog's thumbs), which are on the side of the front legs.

EARS

A Labrador's ears should be clean and odour-free. There are many proprietary ear cleansers and ear wipes available from pet shops; however, the less you put down the dog's ears, the better. A weekly wipe with a tissue should suffice to remove any dirt. Do not poke cotton-buds down the dog's ears. If you see any sign of black wax, or your dog is scratching his ears and shaking his head, you will need to consult a vet.

TEETH

The Labrador has strong, white teeth, which generally stay in

The adult Labrador has a low-maintenance coat but it still requires regular grooming.

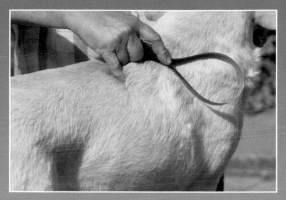

A rake is useful for removing dead hair, particularly when your dog is moulting.

You can use a wide-toothed comb to work through the coat; a narrow-toothed comb will then remove dead hair.

Wipe the ears with a tissue, but do not probe too deeply.

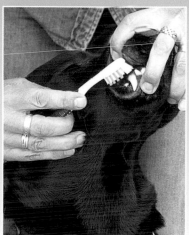

Remember to reward your Labrador after teeth cleaning.

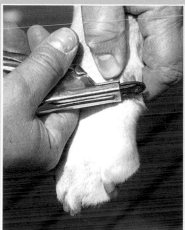

Nails may need regular trimming. The dewclaw (pictured) may also need attention.

good condition throughout his life, with little tartar build-up. Eating dried food, and gnawing bones aids tooth cleansing. If you decide to feed a softer diet, you will probably need to attend to the teeth more often.

If you need to clean your Labrador's teeth, you can buy doggy toothpaste and finger-worn doggy toothbrushes from the pet store. If the teeth become heavily encrusted with tartar, it will need to be removed under sedation by a vet, otherwise gum disease and tooth loss may occur.

PREVENTATIVE HEALTH CARE

PARASITE CONTROL
Your puppy should have been wormed at least three times prior to leaving the breeder, as all puppies are born with roundworms at a larval stage. Advice should be taken from your veterinary surgeon on subsequent worming, but this will probably be at least monthly until the puppy is six months old, and then four times a year.

You also need to ensure that your puppy is free from fleas and other external parasites. Monthly treatment with one of the spot-on treatments is now the easiest way to do this, along with treatment of the environment, as part of the parasite's life stage is off the host. The pup's bed should be treated with a spray (which normally lasts for six months and is designed to arrest the development of the flea egg). It is also important to make frequent use of the vacuum cleaner. Don't forget to vacuum out the car if your dog is a frequent traveller. If you are effective at controlling fleas (and most spot-on products stop lice as well), your dog is unlikely to suffer from tapeworm infection, as the tapeworm requires the presence of fleas or lice to complete its lifecycle. (For more information on internal and external parasites, see Chapter 8.)

VACCINATIONS
Your puppy will need to be vaccinated. Very often the first vaccination will be given by the new owner's veterinary surgeon, who will give advice on what vaccinations are required and when they need to be given. This can be done at the same time as a complete health check of your puppy. This check is reassuring both for the new owner and the breeder, as confirmation of a healthy pup is good news all round. Occasionally the breeder will have organised for the puppy to have had the first of the initial vaccinations. However, this is by no means the norm and it still needs to be followed up with a repeat vaccination. (For more information on vaccinations, see Chapter 8.)

FIRST-AID
The proper and legal person to treat a sick dog is the veterinary surgeon who has the training to make a correct diagnosis and provide the appropriate treatment. However, there are occasions when first-aid treatment needs to be given by the owner prior to taking your Labrador to the vet. The purpose of first-aid is to relieve pain and suffering and to stop the animal's condition getting any worse. Also, some minor conditions can be alleviated if owners take the correct measures. Some of the most common conditions and their first-aid are listed below.

Spot-on treatment for external parasites is easy and effective.

WOUNDS

Cuts may be clean (e.g. where caused by glass) and bleed profusely, which helps remove infection, but important blood vessels may be severed. Jagged cuts (e.g. caused by barbed wire) can become easily infected and are very sore for the dog.

Puncture wounds can be caused by objects penetrating the skin or paw, (e.g. thorns or bites). There is generally not much bleeding unless a major blood vessel is hit. They heal quickly but can harbour infection, which has penetrated the wound on teeth or thorns and can give rise to an abscess. Therefore, prompt veterinary attention is advised.

Treatment

For a straight cut or jagged tear: examine wound, flush and clean with salt water (1 teaspoon to a pint), and cover or bandage if necessary. Fresh air is fine for a clean wound, but if there is a lot of bleeding with, for example, a cut paw, you will need to apply a bandage. If the blood seeps through this, put another one on top and get veterinary attention immediately. Tourniquets are not recommended without specialist training, but you can firmly hold a leg well above a wound to help stem the flow. Always prevent dogs licking at wounds, as this can cause infection.

For puncture wounds: if there is something in it (e.g. a thorn), remove it whole if possible, but otherwise prevent weight bearing and pinpoint the exact location for the vet. Grass seeds are often very difficult to remove and may

A responsible dog owner should learn the basics of first-aid.

break off if you attempt this. Do not try to remove large pieces of wood from wounds, as more damage can be done.

LIMPING

This may be the result of cut paws, bruises, pulled muscles, tendons, or ligaments, bone diseases or back ache.

In the case of fractures and dislocations, the dog will be in a lot of pain. The area will probably look deformed and swollen. If this is the case, immediate veterinary attention should be sought.

Treatment

Examine paws for obvious injury, and, if so, proceed as above. Consider the recent history. Has

the dog jumped awkwardly, for instance? If resting does not improve the condition, veterinary attention should be sought.

BROKEN NAILS OR DEWCLAWS

This is often very painful for the dog but with little bleeding. Where dogs walk regularly on hard ground, it tends to keep most of the nails short. Long nails, particularly on the dewclaws, are more easily broken or knocked out of place.

Treatment

Bath in salt water as above and keep clean. If the pink quick is showing, or the nail is split or coming adrift from the toe or leg, veterinary attention should be sought.

COAT LOSS

This is usually due to moulting. If the dog is groomed well for a few days, the hair loss should stop and any irritation and scratching should also cease.

Hair loss due to parasites is usually coupled with a lot of scratching, with or without sore patches developing.

Allergies can cause hair loss, especially in pale-coloured dogs, who may lick 'hot spots' on the skin. Can also be related to parasites or arthritis when over joints.

Treatment

Groom well if moulting to help remove the dead hair, especially the profuse undercoat. Use a soft plastic or rounded-pin metal comb and bristle or plastic brush.

Seek veterinary attention if normal parasite control has not worked. Never apply a parasite product directly on to sore skin or bare patches.

For sore patches, bathe the affected areas with salt water if necessary. Soothe with some calamine lotion and seek veterinary attention. Prevent the dog continuing to lick or scratch at the sore patches.

SORE EYES

The dog may be reluctant to open the eye and may have a discharge. It can also be caused by small objects entering, penetrating or damaging the eye, as well as infections.

Treatment

Prompt veterinary attention is required, as eyes are delicate. Gently bathe away any discharge with warm water or cold tea.

Keep a close check on your Labrador so you can spot health problems at an early stage.

EAR PROBLEMS

Cuts on the flap are usually noticed when the dog shakes his head a lot, covering everywhere with blood even though often the bleeding is not profuse. However, the shaking often delays healing by continually opening up the cut.

Infections or small objects entering the ear can cause irritation and infection. Infections are usually coupled with smelly ears, which often have a dirty discharge. If left untreated, can also lead to a blood blister forming on the ear flap from continual shaking.

Treatment

Seek veterinary attention if the cut does not heal or if it has made a tear, as the flap may need stitching. Otherwise treat as wounds, above.

Never push objects into the ear in an attempt to clean them. If the dog starts shaking the ear very suddenly, it may mean a grass seed has entered the ear. Seek veterinary attention immediately.

For dirty-looking ears, use a proprietary liquid ear cleaner, as directed, to flush out the 'dirt' over a couple of days. If this does not work, consult the vet. Never put powder in the ears. A swollen blood blister on the ear flap needs veterinary attention.

BEE AND WASP STINGS

Not normally life-threatening unless either the dog swallows the bee and gets stung in the throat and this swells and blocks the airways or the dog is allergic. If the dog collapses, get veterinary help immediately.

Treatment

Bee stings are acid, so bath with a mild alkaline (e.g. bicarbonate of soda solution) to relieve the pain. If the sting can be seen, remove it. Wasp stings are alkaline, so bath with a mild acid (e.g. dilute vinegar or lemon juice) to relieve the pain.

SMELLY BREATH OR BAD TEETH

Seek veterinary attention and advice on treatment and preventative care.

Treatment

Train your dog to have his teeth brushed with a doggy toothpaste (human type not advised).

SICKNESS AND DIARRHOEA

Not uncommon in the dog, who is a natural scavenger. Extra care and prompt veterinary attention is required with old dogs or ones with other known diseases.

Treatment

Withhold food and (unless a geriatric or one with known kidney problems) all but small sips of tepid water. If signs persist after 24 hours, seek veterinary advice. If signs stop, put on a light diet (e.g. white fish or chicken with rice) and gradually wean back on to a normal diet over a few days.

DEAD TAIL

Some Labradors, particularly young ones swimming for the first time, suffer from a dropped tail, which can be uncomfortable. It is thought to be caused by the bellyflop-type action of the outstretched tail slapping the water.

Treatment

The tail generally comes back into use over one or two days. Keep the dog warm and let him sit and move in a manner most comfortable for him. If symptoms persist or the immediate history suggests a more serious injury, obtain veterinary advice.

ANAL GLAND PROBLEMS

Dogs may scoot on their bottom or lick the area under or around the tail and may cause self-inflicted lick sores. The glands (which are either side and just below the anus) may make the area look swollen. Can occur after diarrhoea, as the soft stools do not excrete the glands as firmer ones normally do while being passed.

Treatment

Seek veterinary advice to have the glands emptied and for advice on any subsequent occurrences.

Gland emptying is something that can be learnt by the dog owner if the condition occurs frequently.

CARING FOR THE OLDER DOG

Although the older dog may lose some mobility, it is still important that he has regular daily activity. Two or three 10- to 15-minute walks a day would be ideal, as this keeps the joints mobile. It is also important to keep the oldie's mind alert and keep up his training, such as playing gentle fetch games with a ball or collecting the newspaper. The old adage 'use it or lose it', is as important for dogs as it is for

The older Labrador will slow down, but with good care he will still enjoy a good quality of life.

humans. If the older dog is just kept indoors and occasionally let out into the garden, to relieve himself between bouts of sleeping, he will soon lose his toilet training. He may also become depressed and start moaning or barking.

Feeding a special senior diet from about the age of seven is advisable. Consider feeding a diet with additional additives to help joint mobility, such as green-lipped muscle or cod liver oil. An annual check up with the veterinary surgeon is important to spot any problems at an early stage. The vet can also look at the dog's teeth and take action if necessary, as dental problems are more common in older dogs. In all matters of health care, prevention is better than cure. Your dog will also appreciate a well-padded bed to protect the bony prominences on his body, which can sometimes cause problems in older age. Sometimes the introduction of a new pup can put life back into the older dog, as there is more stimulus in his life. However, make sure that the new pup gives your oldie plenty of time to himself as well.

SAYING GOODBYE

Many owners find it hard to accept that, at some point, they will have to deal with their dog's death. Unfortunately, not many dogs die peacefully in their sleep, which although still upsetting, may be easier for an owner to accept, as they have not had to make the decision to end the dog's life.

What must be remembered is that dogs rely on us to do our best for them. Dogs do not like being unclean in the house, and this is one of the things that can occur towards the end.

Fortunately, dogs do not suffer the same psychological anxiety about medical or other conditions that may ultimately lead to their death. Neither do they have a prior understanding of what is to happen if the time comes when we need to give our biggest gift, and show our greatest love for them, by preventing suffering and allowing the veterinary surgeon to give them their final sleep.

It may be difficult for the veterinary surgeon to be exact about when that time comes, and there are many different scenarios that can lead to the final demise. The problem is that the older the dog gets, the more difficult it is to treat problems with any degree of success. Many of the problems associated with old age can be managed rather than cured.

Once management starts to become very difficult, or impossible, your dog's quality of life has to be considered. You will probably have a better idea than the veterinary surgeon as to whether or not your dog is still enjoying life. A general rule of thumb is: if your Labrador loses his interest in food for more than a temporary period, then he is probably very ill indeed.

On the other hand, it sometimes happens that the dog has a condition that does not worry him too much, but aspects of his condition might cause health (or financial) problems for other humans in the household. For example, a dog that is incurably incontinent might be managed for a period of time if he lives in a house with a good utility area, with direct access to a secure garden, and there are only adults living in the house. However, if he lives in a small house and garden, with young children or crawling babies, it will cause considerable management problems. If this is the case, the owner should not feel guilty for having put the dog to sleep as opposed to confining him to a garden pen or kennel, where he would not be able to understand why he was suddenly excluded from the house.

Every case needs to be considered individually, but never go on so long that your dog suffers at the end. Give him the loving release that fortunately we are able to provide for him, no matter how painful it is for you.

It is important to know when it is time to say goodbye to your beloved Labrador.

TRAINING AND SOCIALISATION

Chapter 6

When you decided to bring a Labrador Retriever into your life, you probably had dreams of how it was going to be: long walks together, cosy evenings with a Lab lying devotedly at your feet, and whenever you returned home, there would always be a special welcome waiting for you.

There is no doubt that you can achieve all this – and much more – with a Labrador, but like anything that is worth having, you must be prepared to put in the work. A Labrador, regardless of whether it is a puppy or an adult, does not come ready trained, understanding exactly what you want and fitting perfectly into your lifestyle. A Labrador has to learn his place in your family and he must discover what is acceptable behaviour.

We have a great starting point in that the Labrador has an outstanding temperament. The breed was developed to be a biddable shooting companion, and all Labradors share a happy, eager-to-please nature. The Labrador is also an intelligent dog, so we have all the ingredients needed to produce a well-trained, well-behaved companion.

THE FAMILY PACK

Dogs have been domesticated for some 14,000 years, but, luckily for us, they have inherited and retained behaviour from their distant ancestor – the wolf. A Labrador Retriever may never have lived in the wild, but he is born with the survival skills and the mentality of a meat-eating predator who hunts in a pack. A wolf living in a pack owes its existence to mutual co-operation and an acceptance of a hierarchy, as this ensures both food and protection. A domesticated dog living in a family pack has exactly the same outlook. He wants food, companionship, and leadership – and it is your job to provide for these needs.

HOW TO BE A GOOD LEADER

There are a number of guidelines to follow to establish yourself in the role of leader in a way that your Labrador understands and respects. If you have a puppy, you may think you don't have to take this on board for a few months, but that would be a big mistake. Start as you mean to go on, and your pup will be quick to find his place in his new family.

- **Keep it simple:** Decide on the rules you want your Labrador to obey and always make it 100 per cent clear what is acceptable, and what is unacceptable, behaviour.
- **Be consistent:** If you are not consistent about enforcing rules, how can you expect your Labrador to take you seriously? There is nothing worse than allowing your Lab to jump up

YOUR ROLE

Theories about dog behaviour and methods of training go in and out of fashion, but in reality, nothing has changed from the day when wolves ventured in from the wild to join the family circle. The wolf (and equally the dog) accepts a subservient place in the family pack in return for food and protection. In a dog's eyes, you are his leader, and he relies on you to make all the important decisions. This does not mean that you have to act like a dictator or a bully. You are accepted as a leader, without argument, as long as you have the right credentials.

The first part of the job is easy. You are the provider, and you are therefore respected because you supply food. In a Labrador's eyes, you must be the ultimate hunter because a day never goes by when you cannot find food. The second part of the leader's job description is straightforward, but for some reason we find it hard to achieve. In order for a dog to accept his place in the family pack he must respect his leader as the decision-maker. A low-ranking pack animal does not question authority; he is perfectly happy to see someone else shoulder the responsibility. Problems will only arise if you cut a poor figure as leader and the dog feels he should mount a challenge for the top-ranking role.

Can you be a firm, fair and consistent leader?

at you one moment and then scolding him the next time he does it because you were wearing your best clothes. As far as the Labrador is concerned, he may as well try it on because he can't predict your reaction.

- **Get your timing right:** If you are rewarding your Labrador, and equally if you are reprimanding him, you must respond within one to two seconds otherwise the dog will not link his behaviour with your reaction (see page 94).

- **Read your dog's body language:** Find out how to read body language and facial expressions (see page 92) so that you understand your Labrador's feelings and his intentions.

- **Be aware of your own body language:** You can help your dog to learn by using your body language to communicate with him. For example, if you want your dog to come to you, open your arms out and look inviting. If you want your dog to stay, use a hand signal (palm flat, facing the dog) so you are effectively 'blocking' his advance.

- **Tone of voice:** Dogs are very receptive to tone of voice, so you can use your voice to praise him or to correct undesirable behaviour. If you are pleased with your Labrador, praise him to the skies in a warm, happy voice. If you want to stop him raiding the bin, use a deep, stern voice when you say "No".

- **Give one command only:** If you keep repeating a

Your Labrador understands body language better than verbal commands.

command, or keep changing it, your Labrador will think you are babbling and will probably ignore you. If your Labrador does not respond the first time you ask, make it simple by using a treat to lure him into position, and then you can reward him for a correct response.

- **Daily reminders:** A young, exuberant Lab is apt to forget his manners from time to time, and an adolescent dog may attempt to challenge your authority (see page 103). Rather than coming down on your Labrador like a ton of bricks when he does something wrong, try to

prevent bad manners by daily reminders of good manners. For example:

- Do not let your dog barge ahead of you when you are going through a door.
- Do not let him leap out of the car the moment you open the door (which could be potentially lethal, as well as being disrespectful).
- Do not let him eat from your hand when you are at the table.
- Do not let him 'win' a toy at the end of a play session and then make off with it. You 'own' his toys, and you must end every play session on your terms.

91

UNDERSTANDING YOUR LABRADOR

Body language is an important means of communication between dogs, which they use to make friends, to assert status, and to avoid conflict. It is important to get on your dog's wavelength by understanding his body language and reading his facial expressions.

- A positive body posture and a wagging tail indicate a happy, confident dog.
- A crouched body posture with ears back and tail down show that a dog is being submissive. A dog may do this when he is being told off or if a more assertive dog approaches him.
- A bold dog will stand tall, looking strong and alert. His ears will be forward and his tail will be held high.
- A dog who raises his hackles (lifting the fur along his topline) is trying to look as scary as possible. This may be the prelude to aggressive behaviour, but, in many cases, the dog is apprehensive and is unsure how to cope with a situation.
- A playful dog will go down on his front legs while standing on his hind legs in a bow position. This friendly invitation says: "I'm no threat, let's play."
- A dominant, aggressive dog will meet other dogs with a hard stare. If he is challenged, he may bare his teeth and growl, and the corners of his mouth will be drawn forward. His ears will be forward and he will appear tense in every muscle (see page 108).
- A nervous dog will often show aggressive behaviour as a means of self-protection. If threatened, this dog will lower his head and flatten his ears. The corners of his mouth may be drawn back, and he may bark or whine.
- Some dogs are 'smilers', curling up their top lip and showing their teeth when they greet people. This should never be confused with a snarl, which would be accompanied by the upright posture of a dominant dog. A smiling dog will have a low body posture and a wagging tail; he is being submissive and it is a greeting that is often used when low-ranking animals greet high-ranking animals in a pack.

You can see that these two Labradors are happy and relaxed with each other, and there is no hint of nervousness or aggression.

GIVING REWARDS

Why should your Labrador do as you ask? If you follow the guidelines given above, your Labrador should respect your authority, but what about the time when he is playing with a new doggy friend or has found a really enticing scent? The answer is that you must always be the most interesting, the most attractive, and the most irresistible person in your Labrador's eyes. It would be nice to think you could achieve this by personality alone, but most of us need a little extra help. You need to find out what is the biggest reward for your dog – in a Labrador's case, it will nearly always be food – and to give him a treat when he does as you ask. For some dogs, the reward might be a play with a favourite toy, but, whatever it is, it must be something that your dog really wants.

When you are teaching a dog a new exercise, you should reward him frequently. When he knows the exercise or command, reward him randomly so that he keeps on responding to you in a positive manner. If your dog does something extra special, like leaving his canine chum mid-play in the park, make sure he really knows how pleased you are by giving him a handful of treats or throwing his ball a few extra times. If he gets a bonanza reward, he is more likely to come back on future occasions, because you have proved to be even more rewarding than his previous activity.

In order to train your Labrador, you need to understand how his mind works.

TOP TREATS

Some trainers grade treats depending on what they are asking the dog to do. A dog may get a low-grade treat, such as a piece of dry food, to reward good behaviour on a random basis, such as sitting when you open a door or allowing you to examine his teeth. But high-grade treats, which may be cooked liver, sausage or cheese, are reserved for training new exercises or for use in the park when you want a really good recall. Whatever type of treat you use, remember to subtract it from your Labrador's daily ration. Fat Labs are lethargic, prone to health problems, and will almost certainly have a shorter life expectancy. Reward your Labrador, but always keep a check on his figure!

HOW DO DOGS LEARN?

It is not difficult to get inside your Labrador's head and understand how he learns, as it is not dissimilar to the way we learn. Dogs learn by conditioning: they find out that specific behaviours produce specific consequences. This is known as operant conditioning or consequence

THE CLICKER REVOLUTION

Karen Pryor pioneered the technique of clicker training when she was working with dolphins. It is very much a continuation of Pavlov's work and makes full use of association learning.

Karen wanted to mark 'correct' behaviour at the precise moment it happened. She found it was impossible to toss a fish to a dolphin when it was in mid-air, when she wanted to reward it. Her aim was to establish a conditioned response so the dolphin knew that it had performed correctly and a reward would follow.

The solution was the clicker: a small matchbox-shaped training aid, with a metal tongue that makes a click when it is pressed. To begin with, the dolphin had to learn that a click meant that food was coming. The dolphin then learnt that it must 'earn' a click in order to get a reward. Clicker training has been used with many different animals, most particularly with dogs, and it has proved hugely successful. It is a great aid for pet owners and is also widely used by professional trainers who train highly specialised skills.

learning. Consequences have to be immediate or clearly linked to the behaviour, as a dog sees the world in terms of action and result. Dogs will quickly learn if an action has a bad consequence or a good consequence.

Dogs also learn by association. This is known as classical conditioning or association learning. It is the type of learning made famous by Pavlov's experiment with dogs. Pavlov presented dogs with food and measured their salivary response (how much they drooled). Then he rang a bell just before presenting the food. At first, the dogs did not salivate until the food was presented. But after a while they learnt that the sound of the bell meant that food was coming, and so they salivated when they heard the bell. A dog needs to learn the association in order for it to have any meaning. For example, a dog that has never seen a lead before will be completely indifferent to it. A dog that has learnt that a lead means he is going for a walk will get excited the second he sees the lead; he has learnt to associate a lead with a walk.

BE POSITIVE
The most effective method of training dogs is to use their ability to learn by consequence and to teach that the behaviour you want produces a good consequence. For example, if you ask your Labrador to "Sit", and reward him with a treat, he will learn that it is worth his while to sit on command because it will lead to an enjoyable reward. He is far more likely to repeat the behaviour, and the behaviour will become stronger, because it results in a positive outcome. This method of training is known as positive reinforcement, and it generally leads to a happy, co-operative dog that is willing to work, and a handler who has fun training their dog.

The opposite approach is negative reinforcement. This is far less effective and often results in a poor relationship between dog and owner. In this method of training, you ask your Labrador to "Sit", and, if he does not respond, you deliver a sharp yank on the training collar or push his rear to the ground. The dog learns that not responding to your command has a bad consequence, and he may be less likely to ignore you in the future. However, it may well have a bad consequence for you, too. A dog that is treated in this way may associate harsh handling with the handler and become aggressive or fearful. Instead of establishing a pattern of willing co-operation, you are establishing a relationship built on coercion.

GETTING STARTED

As you train your Labrador, you will develop your own techniques as you get to know what motivates him. You may decide to get involved with clicker training or you may prefer to go for a simple command-and-reward formula. It does not matter what form of training you use, as long as it is based on positive, reward-based methods.

There are a few important guidelines to bear in mind when you are training your Labrador:

- Find a training area that is free from distractions, particularly when you are just starting out.
- Keep training sessions short, especially with young puppies that have very short attention spans.
- Do not train if you are in a bad mood or if you are on a tight

A puppy has a short concentration span, so keep training sessions short and positive.

schedule – the training session will be doomed to failure.
- If you are using a toy as a reward, make sure it is only available when you are training. In this way it has an added value for your Labrador.
- If you are using food treats, make sure they are bite-size and easy to swallow; you don't want to hang about while your Lab chews on his treat.

- All food treats must be deducted from your Labrador's daily food ration.
- When you are training, move around your allocated area so that your dog does not think that an exercise can only be performed in one place.
- If your Labrador is finding an exercise difficult, try not to get frustrated. Go back a step and praise him for his effort. You

will probably find he is more successful when you try again at the next training session.

- Always end training sessions on a happy, positive note. Ask your Labrador to do something you know he can do – it could be a trick he enjoys performing – and then reward him with a few treats or an extra-long play session.

In the exercises that follow, clicker training is introduced and followed, but all the exercises will work without the use of a clicker.

INTRODUCING A CLICKER

This is dead easy, and your ever-hungry Labrador will learn about the clicker in record time! It can be combined with attention training, which is a very useful tool and can be used on many different occasions.

- Prepare some treats and go to an area that is free from distractions. When your Labrador stops sniffing around and looks at you, click and reward by throwing him a treat. This means he will not crowd you, but will go looking for the treat. Repeat a couple of times. If your Lab is very easily distracted, you may need to start this exercise with the dog on a lead.

- After a few clicks, your Labrador understands that if he hears a click, he will get a treat. He must now learn that he must 'earn' a click. This time, when your Labrador looks at you, wait a little longer before clicking, and then reward him. If your Lab is on a lead but responding well, try him off lead.

- When your Labrador is working for a click and giving you his attention, you can introduce a cue or command word, such as "Watch". Repeat a few times, using the cue. You now have a Lab that understands the clicker and will give you his attention when you ask him to "Watch".

TRAINING EXERCISES

THE SIT

This is the easiest exercise to teach, so it is rewarding for both you and your Labrador.

- Choose a tasty treat and hold it just above your puppy's nose. As he looks up at the treat, he will naturally go into the Sit. As soon as he is in position, reward him.

- Repeat the exercise, and when your pup understands what you want, introduce the "Sit" command.

- You can practise at mealtimes by holding out the bowl and waiting for your dog to sit. Most Labradors learn this one very quickly!

To start with, you will need to lure your Labrador into the Sit position. But soon he will respond to a verbal command alone.

When a treat is lured to the ground, your Labrador will follow it and go into the Down position.

Recall should always be treated as a fun exercise, so give your dog lots of encouragement and praise.

THE DOWN

Work hard at this exercise because a reliable Down is useful in many different situations, and an instant Down can be a lifesaver.

- You can start with your dog in a Sit, or it is just as effective to teach it when the dog is standing. Hold a treat just below your puppy's nose and slowly lower it towards the ground. The treat acts as a lure, and your puppy will follow it, first going down on this forequarters, and then bringing his hindquarters down as he tries to get the treat.
- Make sure you close your fist around the treat, and only reward your puppy with the treat when he is in the correct position. If your puppy is reluctant to go Down, you can apply gentle pressure on his shoulders to encourage him to go into the correct position.
- When your puppy is following the treat and going in to position, introduce a verbal command.
- Build up this exercise over a period of time, each time waiting a little longer before giving the reward, so the puppy learns to stay in the Down position.

THE RECALL

It is never too soon to start training the Recall. In fact, if you have a puppy it is best to start almost from the moment the puppy arrives home, as he has a strong instinct to follow you. Make sure you are always happy and excited when your Labrador comes to you, even if he has been slower than you would like. Your Labrador must believe that the greatest reward is coming to you.

- You can start teaching the Recall from the moment your puppy arrives home. He will naturally follow you, so keep calling his name, and reward him when he comes to you.
- Practise in the garden, and when your puppy is busy exploring, get his attention by calling his name. As he runs towards you, introduce the verbal command "Come". Make sure you sound happy and

exciting, so your puppy wants to come to you. When he responds, give him lots of praise.

- If your puppy is slow to respond, try running away a few paces, or jumping up and down. It doesn't matter how silly you look, the key issue is to get your puppy's attention, and then make yourself irresistible!

- In a dog's mind, coming when called should be regarded as the best fun because he knows he is always going to be rewarded. Never make the mistake of telling your dog off, no matter how slow he is to respond, as you will undo all your previous hard work.

- When you are free-running your dog, make sure you have his favourite toy or a pocket full of treats so you can reward him at intervals throughout the walk when you call him to you. Do not allow your dog to run free and only call him back at the end of the walk to clip his lead on. An intelligent Labrador will soon realise that the Recall means the end of his walk and the end of fun – so who can blame him for not wanting to come back?

TRAINING LINE

This is the equivalent of a very long lead, which you can buy at a pet store, or you can make your own with a length of rope. The training line is attached to your Labrador's collar and should be around 15 feet (4.5 metres) in length.

The purpose of the training line is to prevent your Labrador from disobeying you so that he never has the chance to get into bad habits. For example, when you call your Lab and he ignores you, you can immediately pick up the end of the training line and call him again. By picking up the line you will have attracted his attention, and if you call in an excited, happy voice, your Lab will come to you. The moment he comes to you, give him a tasty treat so he is instantly rewarded for making the 'right' decision.

The training line is very useful when your Lab becomes an adolescent and is testing your leadership. When you have

SECRET WEAPON

You can build up a strong Recall by using another form of association learning. Buy a whistle, and when you are giving your Lab his food, peep on the whistle. You can choose the type of signal you want to give: two short peeps or one long whistle, for example. Within a matter of days, your dog will learn that the sound of the whistle means that food is coming.

Now transfer the lesson outside. Arm yourself with some tasty treats and the whistle. Allow your Lab to run free in the garden, and, after a couple of minutes, use the whistle. The dog has already learnt to associate the whistle with food, so he will come towards you. Immediately reward him with a treat and lots of praise. Repeat the lesson a few times in the garden so you are confident that your dog is responding before trying it in the park. Make sure you always have some treats in your pocket when you go for a walk, and your dog will quickly learn how rewarding it is to come to you.

reinforced the correct behaviour a number of times, your dog will build up a strong recall and you will not need to use a training line.

WALKING ON A LOOSE LEAD

This is a simple exercise, which baffles many Labrador owners. In most cases, owners are too impatient, wanting to get on with the expedition rather that training the dog how to walk on a lead. Take time with this one; the Labrador is a strong dog, and a Labrador that pulls on the lead is no pleasure to own.

- In the early stages of lead training, allow your puppy to pick his route and follow him. He will get used to the feeling of being 'attached' to you and has no reason to put up any resistance.
- Next, find a toy or a tasty treat and show it to your puppy. Let him follow the follow the treat/toy for a few paces, and then reward him.
- Build up the amount of time your pup will walk with you, and when he is walking nicely by your side, introduce the verbal command "Heel" or "Close". Give lots of praise when your pup is in the correct position.
- When your pup is walking alongside you, keep focusing his attention on you by using his name and then rewarding him when he looks at you. If it is going well, introduce some changes of direction.
- Do not attempt to take your puppy out on the lead until you have mastered the basics at home. You need to be

This Labrador has learnt to walk on a loose lead, focusing his attention on his owner when requested.

confident that your puppy accepts the lead and will focus his attention on you, when requested, before you face the challenge of a busy environment.

- As your Labrador gets bigger and stronger, he may try to pull on the lead, particularly if you are heading somewhere he wants to go, such as the park. If this happens, stop, call your dog to you, and do not set off again until he is in the correct position. It may take time, but

your Labrador will eventually realise that it is more productive to walk by your side than to pull ahead.

STAYS

This may not be the most exciting exercise, but it is one of the most useful. There are many occasions when you want your Labrador to stay in position, even if it is only for a few seconds. The classic example is when you want your Labrador to stay in the back of the car until you have clipped his

Give a positive hand signal so your Labrador understands that he is to stay in position.

lead on. Some trainers use the verbal command "Stay" when the dog is to stay in position for an extended period of time, and "Wait" if the dog is to stay in position for a few seconds until you give the next command. Other trainers use a universal "Stay" to cover all situations. It all comes down to personal preference, and as long as you are consistent, your dog will understand the command he is given.

- Put your puppy in a Sit or a Down, and use a hand signal (flat palm, facing the dog) to show he is to stay in position.

Step a pace away from the dog. Wait a second, step back and reward him. If you have a lively pup, you may find it easier to train this exercise on the lead.
- Repeat the exercise, gradually increasing the distance you can leave your dog. When you return to your dog's side, praise him quietly, and release him with a command, such as "OK".
- Remember to keep your body language very still when you are training this exercise, and avoid eye contact with your dog. Work on this exercise over a period of time, and you will build up a really reliable Stay.

SOCIALISATION

While your Labrador is mastering basic obedience exercises, there is other, equally important, work to do with him. A Labrador is not only becoming a part of your home and family, he is becoming a member of the community. He needs to be able to live in the outside world, coping calmly with every new situation that comes his way. It is your job to introduce him to as many different experiences as possible, and encourage him to behave in an appropriate manner.

In order to socialise your Labrador effectively, it is helpful to understand how his brain is developing, and then you will get a perspective on how he sees the world.

CANINE SOCIALISATION
(Birth to 7 weeks)
This is the time when a dog learns how to be a dog. By interacting with his mother and his littermates, a young pup learns about leadership and submission. He learns to read body posture so that he understands the intentions of his mother and his siblings. A puppy that is taken away from his litter too early may always have behavioural problems with other dogs, either being fearful or aggressive.

SOCIALISATION PERIOD
(7 to 12 weeks)
This is the time to get cracking and introduce your Lab puppy to as many different experiences as possible. This includes meeting different people, other dogs and animals, seeing new sights, and hearing a range of sounds, from

Every new situation a puppy finds himself in provides a learning opportunity.

the vacuum cleaner to the roar of traffic. At this stage, a puppy learns very quickly and what he learns will stay with him for the rest of his life. This is the best time for a puppy to move to a new home, as he is adaptable and ready to form deep bonds.

*FEAR-IMPRINT PERIOD
(8 to 11 weeks)*
This occurs during the socialisation period, and it can be the cause of problems if it is not handled carefully. If a pup is exposed to a frightening or painful experience, it will lead to lasting impressions. Obviously, you will attempt to avoid frightening situations, such as your pup being bullied by a mean-spirited older dog, or a

firework going off, but you cannot always protect your puppy from the unexpected. If your pup has a nasty experience, the best plan is to make light of it and distract him by offering him a treat or a game. The pup will take the lead from you and will be reassured that there is nothing to worry about. If you mollycoddle him and sympathise with him, he is far more likely to retain the memory of his fear.

*SENIORITY PERIOD
(12 to 16 weeks)*
During this period, your Lab puppy starts to cut the apron strings and becomes more independent. He will test out his status to find out who is the pack leader: him or you. Bad habits,

such as play biting, which may have been seen as endearing a few weeks earlier, should be firmly discouraged. Remember to use positive, reward-based training, but make sure your puppy knows that you are the leader and must be respected.

*SECOND FEAR-IMPRINT PERIOD
(6 to 14 months)*
This period is not as critical as the first fear-imprint period, but it should still be handled carefully. During this time your Lab may appear apprehensive, or he may show fear of something familiar. You may feel as if you have taken a backwards step, but if you adopt a calm, positive manner, your Lab will see that there is nothing to be frightened

A well-socialised Labrador will be calm and confident, and can be trusted in a variety of different situations.

again and may become aggressive towards other dogs. Firmness and continued training are essential at this time so that your Labrador accepts his status in the family pack.

IDEAS FOR SOCIALISATION

When you are socialising your Labrador, you want him to experience as many different situations as possible. Try out some of the following ideas, which will ensure your Lab has an all-round education.

If you are taking on a rescued dog and have little knowledge of his background, it is important to work through a programme of socialisation. A young puppy soaks up new experiences like a sponge, but an older dog can still learn. If a rescued dog shows fear or apprehension, treat him in exactly the same way as you would treat a youngster who is going through the second fear-imprint period (see page 101).

- Accustom your puppy to household noises, such as the vacuum cleaner, the television and the washing machine.
- Ask visitors to come to the door, wearing different types of clothing – for example, wearing a hat, a long raincoat, or carrying a stick or an umbrella.
- If you do not have children at home, make sure your Lab has a chance to meet and play with them. Go to a local park and watch children in the play area. You will not be able to take your Labrador inside the play area, but he will see children playing and will get used to their shouts of excitement.

of. Do not make your dog confront the thing that frightens him. Simply distract his attention, and give him something else to think about, such as obeying a simple command, such as "Sit" or "Down". This will give you the opportunity to praise and reward your dog, and will help to boost his confidence.

YOUNG ADULTHOOD AND MATURITY (1 to 4 years)

The timing of this phase depends on the size of the dog: the bigger the dog, the later it is. This period coincides with a dog's increased size and strength, mental as well as physical. Some dogs, particularly those with a dominant nature, will test your leadership

- Attend puppy classes. These are designed for puppies between the ages of 12 to 20 weeks, and they give puppies a chance to play and interact together in a controlled, supervised environment. Your vet will have details of a local class.
- Take a walk around some quiet streets, such as a residential area, so your Lab can get used to the sound of traffic. As he becomes more confident, progress to busier areas.
- Go to a railway station. You don't have to get on a train if you don't need to, but your Labrador will have the chance to experience trains, people wheeling luggage, loudspeaker announcements, and going up and down stairs and over railway bridges.
- If you live in the town, plan a trip to the country. You can enjoy a day out and provide an opportunity for your Labrador to see livestock, such as sheep, cattle and horses.
- One of the best places for socialising a dog is at a country fair. There will be crowds of people, livestock in pens, tractors, bouncy castles, fairground rides and food stalls.
- When your dog is over 20 weeks of age, find a training class for adult dogs. You may find that your local training class has both puppy and adult classes.

TRAINING CLUBS

There are lots of training clubs to choose from. Your vet will probably have details of clubs in your area, or you can ask friends who have dogs if they attend a

An adolescent Labrador will test the boundaries as he matures into adulthood.

club. Alternatively, use the internet to find out more information. But how do you know if the club is any good?

Before you take your dog, ask if you can go to a class as an observer and find out the following:
- What experience does the instructor(s) have?
- Do they have experience with Labradors?
- Is the class well organised, and are the dogs reasonably quiet? (A noisy class indicates an unruly atmosphere, which will not be conducive to learning.)
- Are there are a number of

classes to suit dogs of different ages and abilities?
- Are positive, reward-based training methods used?
- Does the club train for the Good Citizen Scheme (see page 109).

If you are not happy with the training club, find another one. An inexperienced instructor who cannot handle a number of dogs in a confined environment can do more harm than good.

THE ADOLESCENT LABRADOR

It happens to every dog – and every owner. One minute you

have an obedient well-behaved youngster, and the next you have a boisterous adolescent who appears to have forgotten everything he learnt. This applies equally to males and females, although the type of adolescent behaviour, and its onset, varies between individuals.

In most cases a Labrador male will hit adolescence at around 11 months, and you can expect behavioural changes for at least a couple of months. In most cases, a male Lab will not change dramatically in personality at this time. He will be his usual loving self, but he may be more active and bouncy, and he will misbehave as he tests the boundaries. Female Labradors show adolescent behaviour as they approach their first season; yellow Labs come into season at around eight months, black Labs tend to be a little older. At this time, a female Lab may become a little distant and appear somewhat preoccupied. It is not unlike a woman suffering from PMT. In reality, adolescence is not the nightmare period you may imagine, if you see it from your Labrador's perspective.

Just like a teenager, an adolescent Labrador feels the need to flex his muscles and challenge the status quo. He may become disobedient and break house rules as he tests your authority and your role as leader. Your response must be firm, fair and consistent. If you show that you are a strong leader (see page 90) and are quick to reward good behaviour, your Labrador will accept you as his protector and provider.

WHEN THINGS GO WRONG

Positive, reward-based training has proved to be the most effective method of teaching dogs, but what happens when your Labrador does something wrong and you need to show him that his behaviour is unacceptable? The old-fashioned school of dog training used to rely on the powers of punishment and negative reinforcement. A dog who raided the bin, for example, was smacked. Now we have learnt that it is not only unpleasant and cruel to hit a dog, it is also ineffective. If you hit a dog for stealing, he is more than likely to see you as the bad consequence of stealing, so he may raid the bin again, but probably not when you are around. If he raided the bin some time before you discovered it, he will be even more confused by your punishment, as he will not relate your response to his 'crime'.

A more commonplace example is when a dog fails to respond to a recall in the park. When the dog eventually comes back, the owner puts the dogs on the lead and goes straight home to punish the dog for his poor response. Unfortunately, the dog will have a different interpretation. He does

Over-exuberance is common in young Labradors.

not think: "I won't ignore a recall command because the bad consequence is the end of my play in the park." He thinks: "Coming to my owner resulted in the end of playtime – therefore coming to my owner has a bad consequence, so I won't do that again."

There are a number of strategies to tackle undesirable behaviour – and they have nothing to do with harsh handling.

Ignoring bad behaviour: A lot of undesirable behaviour in young Labradors is to do with over-exuberance. This trait is part of the breed's charm, but it can lead to difficult and sometimes dangerous situations. For example, a young Labrador that repeatedly jumps up at visitors will eventually knock someone over unless he is stopped. In this case, the Labrador is seeking attention, and so the best plan is to ignore him. Do not look at him, do not speak to him, and do not push him down – all these actions are rewarding for your Labrador. But someone who turns their back on him and offers no response is plain boring. The moment your Labrador has four feet on the ground, give him lots of praise and maybe a treat. If you repeat this often enough, the Labrador will learn that jumping up does not have any good consequences, such as getting attention. Instead he is ignored. However, when he has all four feet on the ground, he gets loads of attention. He links the action with the consequence, and chooses the action that is most rewarding. You will find that this strategy works well with all attention-seeking behaviour, such as barking,

whining or scrabbling at doors. Being ignored is a worst-case scenario for a Labrador, so remember to use it as an effective training tool.

Stopping bad behaviour: There are occasions when you want to call an instant halt to whatever it is your Labrador is doing. He may have just jumped on the sofa, or you may have caught him red-handed in the rubbish bin. He has already committed the 'crime', so your aim is to stop him and to redirect his attention. You can do this by using a deep, firm tone of voice to say "No", which will startle him, and then call him to you in a bright, happy voice. If necessary, you can attract him with a toy or a treat. The moment your Labrador stops the undesirable behaviour and comes towards you, you can reward his good behaviour. You can back this up by running through a couple of simple exercises, such as a Sit or a Down, and rewarding with treats. In this way, your Labrador focuses his attention on you, and

sees you as the greatest source of reward and pleasure.

In a more extreme situation, when you want to interrupt undesirable behaviour, and you know that a simple "No" will not do the trick, you can try something a little more dramatic. If you get a can and fill it with pebbles, it will make a really loud noise when you shake it or throw it. The same effect can be achieved with purpose-made training discs. The dog will be startled and stop what he is doing. Even better, the dog will not associate the unpleasant noise with you. This gives you the perfect opportunity to be the nice guy, calling the dog to you and giving him lots of praise.

PROBLEM BEHAVIOUR

If you have trained your Labrador from puppyhood, survived his adolescence and established yourself as a fair and consistent leader, you will end up with a brilliant companion dog. The Labrador is a well-balanced dog who is biddable, eager to please,

If you catch your Labrador red-handed, use a deep, firm voice to startle him.

and rarely has hang-ups. Most Labradors share an exuberant love of life and thrive on spending time with their owners.

However, problems may arise unexpectedly, or you may have taken on a rescued Labrador that has established behavioural problems. If you are worried about your Labrador and feel out of your depth, do not delay in seeking professional help. This is readily available, usually through a referral from your vet, or you can find out additional information on the internet (see Appendices for web addresses). An animal behaviourist will have experience in tackling problem behaviour and will be able to help both you and your dog.

SEPARATION ANXIETY

The Labrador is generally a laid-back character, and if he is brought up to accept short periods of separation from his owner, there is no reason why he should become anxious. A new puppy should be left for short periods on his own, ideally in a crate where he cannot get up to any mischief. It is a good idea to leave him with a boredom-busting toy (see page 57) so he will be happily occupied in your absence. When you return, do not rush to the crate and make a huge fuss. Wait a few minutes, and then calmly go to the crate and release your dog, telling him how good he has been. If this scenario is repeated a number of times, your

Labrador will soon learn that being left on his own is no big deal.

Problems with separation anxiety are most likely to arise if you take on a rescued dog who has major insecurities. You may also find that your Labrador hates being left if you have failed to accustom him to short periods of isolation when he was growing up. Separation anxiety is expressed in a number of ways, and all are equally distressing for both dog and owner. An anxious dog who is left alone may bark and whine continuously, urinate and defecate, and may be extremely destructive.

There are a number of steps you can take when attempting to solve this problem.

- Put up a baby-gate between adjoining rooms, and leave your dog in one room while you are in the other room. Your dog will be able to see you and hear you, but he is learning to cope without being right next to you. Build up the amount of time you can leave your dog in easy stages.
- Buy some boredom-busting toys and fill them with some tasty treats. Whenever you leave your dog, give him a food-filled toy so that he is busy while you are away.
- If you have not used a crate before, it is not too late to start. Make sure the crate is big and comfortable, and train your Labrador to get used to going in his crate while you are in the same room. Gradually build up the amount of time he spends in the crate, and then start leaving the room for short

A boredom-busting toy, filled with food, will help to keep your Labrador occupied.

periods. When you return, do not make a fuss of your dog. Leave him for five or 10 minutes before releasing him so that he gets used to your comings and goings.

- Pretend to go out, putting on your coat and jangling keys, but do not leave the house. An anxious dog often becomes hyped up by the ritual of leave taking, and so this will help to desensitise him.
- When you go out, leave a radio or a TV on. Some dogs are comforted by hearing voices and background noise when they are left alone.
- Try to make your absences as short as possible when you are first training your dog to accept being on his own. When you return, do not fuss your dog, rushing to his crate to release him. Leave him for a few minutes, and when you go to him remain calm and relaxed so that he does not become hyped up with a huge greeting.

If you take these steps, your dog should become less anxious, and, over a period of time, you should be able to solve the problem. However, if you are failing to make progress, do not delay in calling in expert help.

ASSERTIVE BEHAVIOUR
If you have trained and socialised your Labrador correctly, he will know his place in the family pack and will have no desire to challenge your authority. As we have seen, adolescent dogs test the boundaries, and this is the time to enforce all your earlier training so your Labrador accepts

that he is not top dog.

Labradors were bred to be biddable, so it is rare for a Labrador to be over-assertive. However, if you have taken on a rescued dog who has not been trained and socialised, or if you have let your adolescent Labrador rule the roost, you may find you have problems with an over-assertive dog. In most cases, it will be males that try to get the upper hand.

Assertive behaviour is expressed in many different ways, which may include the following:

- Showing lack of respect for your personal space. For example, your dog will barge through doors ahead of you or jump up at you.

- Getting up on to the sofa or your favourite armchair, and growling when you tell him to get back on the floor.
- Guarding a toy or his food bowl by growling when you get too close.
- Growling when anyone approaches his bed or when anyone gets too close to where he is lying.
- Ignoring basic obedience commands.
- Showing no respect to younger members of the family, pushing amongst them and completely ignoring them.
- Male dogs may start marking (cocking their leg) in the house.
- Aggression towards people (see page 108).

A bored Labrador is more likely to show problematic behaviour, so it is important to keep your dog mentally stimulated.

If you see signs of your Labrador becoming too assertive, you must work at lowering his status so that he realises that you are the leader and he must accept your authority. Although you need to be firm, you also need to use positive training methods so that your Labrador is rewarded for the behaviour you want. In this way, his 'correct' behaviour will be strengthened and repeated.

There are a number of steps you can take to lower your Labrador's status. They include:

Teach your Labrador to "Wait" at doorways, so that he allows you to go first.

- Go back to basics and hold daily training sessions. Make sure you have some really tasty treats, or find a toy your Labrador really values and only bring it out at training sessions. Run through all the training exercises you have taught your Labrador. Make a big fuss of him and reward him when he does well. This will reinforce the message that you are the leader and that it is rewarding to do as you ask.
- Teach your Labrador something new; this can be as simple as learning a trick, such as shaking paws. Having something new to think about will mentally stimulate your Labrador, and he will benefit from interacting with you.
- Be 100 per cent consistent with all house rules – your Labrador must never sit on the sofa, and you must never allow him to jump up at you.
- If your Labrador has been guarding his food bowl, put the bowl down empty, and drop in a little food at a time. Periodically stop dropping in the food, and tell your Labrador to "Sit" and "Wait". Wait a few seconds and then reward him by dropping in more food. This shows your Labrador that you are the provider of the food, and he can only eat when you allow him to.
- Make sure the family eats before you feed your Labrador. Some trainers advocate eating in front of the dog (maybe just a few bites from a biscuit) before starting a training session, so the dog appreciates your elevated status.

- Do not let your Labrador barge through doors ahead of you, or leap from the back of the car before you release him. You may need to put your dog on the lead and teach him to "Wait" at doorways, and then reward him for letting you go through first.

If your Labrador is progressing well with his retraining programme, think about getting involved with a dog sport, such as agility or competitive obedience. This will give your Labrador a positive outlet for his energies. However, if your Labrador is still seeking to be too assertive, or you have any other concerns, do not delay in seeking the help of an animal behaviourist.

AGGRESSION

Aggression is a complex issue, as there are different causes and the behaviour may be triggered by numerous factors. It may be directed towards people, but far more commonly it is directed towards other dogs. Aggression in dogs may be the result of:
- Assertive behaviour (see page 107).
- Defensive behaviour: This may be induced by fear, pain or punishment.
- Territory: A dog may become aggressive if strange dogs or people enter his territory (which is generally seen as the house and garden).
- Intra-sexual issues: This is aggression between sexes – male-to-male or female-to-female.
- Parental instinct: A mother dog may become aggressive if she is protecting her puppies.

A well-socialised dog who has had sufficient exposure to other dogs at significant stages of his development will rarely be aggressive. A well-bred Labrador, reared correctly, should not have a hint of aggression in his temperament. Obviously if you have taken on an older, rescued dog, you will have little or no knowledge of his background, and if he shows signs of aggression, the cause will need to be determined. In most cases, you would be well advised to call in professional help if you see aggressive behaviour in your dog; if the aggression is directed towards people, you should seek immediate advice. This behaviour can escalate very quickly and could lead to disastrous consequences.

NEW CHALLENGES
If you enjoy training your Labrador, you may want to try one of the many dog sports that are now on offer.

GOOD CITIZEN SCHEME
This is a scheme run by the Kennel Club in the UK and the American Kennel Club in the USA. The schemes promote responsible ownership and help you to train a well-behaved dog who will fit in with the community. The schemes are excellent for all pet owners, and they are also a good starting point if you plan to compete with your Labrador when he is older. The KC and the AKC schemes vary in format. In the UK there are three levels: bronze, silver and gold, with each test becoming progressively more demanding. In the AKC scheme there is a single test.

Labradors are very successful at therapy work.

Some of the exercises include:
- Walking on a loose lead among people and other dogs.
- Recall amid distractions.
- A controlled greeting where dogs stay under control while owners meet.
- The dog allows all-over grooming and handling by its owner, and also accepts being handled by the examiner.
- Stays, with the owner in sight, and then out of sight.
- Food manners, allowing the owner to eat without begging, and taking a treat on command.
- Sendaway – sending the dog to his bed.

The tests are designed to show the control you have over your dog, and his ability to respond correctly and remain calm in all situations. The Good Citizen Scheme is taught at most training clubs. For more information, log on to the Kennel Club or AKC website (see Appendices).

THERAPY DOGS
The Labrador is ideally suited to working as a therapy dog; he is gentle, kind and lovable. Therapy dogs go with their owners to visit residents in a variety of different institutions, which may include hospitals, care homes, and prisons. It is widely acknowledged that interacting with a dog has great therapeutic benefits, and so the work is very rewarding. Therapy dogs are assessed to ensure they have the correct temperament, and their owners must have a good measure of control. For more information on training your Labrador to be a therapy dog, see Appendices.

SHOWING
In your eyes, your Labrador is the most beautiful dog in the world – but would a judge agree? Showing is a highly competitive sport and as the Labrador is so popular, classes tend to be very big. However, many owners get bitten

Showing is a highly competitive hobby – but it can be very rewarding.

by the showing bug, and their calendar is governed by the dates of the top showing fixtures.

To be successful in the show ring, a Labrador must conform as closely as possible to the Breed Standard, which is a written blueprint describing the 'perfect' Labrador (see Chapter 7). To get started you need to buy a puppy that has show potential and then train him to perform in the ring. A Labrador will be expected to stand in show pose, gait for the judge in order to show off his natural movement, and to be examined by the judge. This involves a detailed hands-on examination, so your Labrador must be bombproof when handled by strangers.

Many training clubs hold ringcraft classes, which are run by experienced showgoers. At these classes, you will learn how to handle your Labrador in the ring, and you will also find out about rules, procedures and show ring etiquette.

The best plan is to start off at some small, informal shows where

you can practise and learn the tricks of the trade before graduating to bigger shows. It's a long haul starting in the very first puppy class, but the dream is to make your Labrador up into a Show Champion.

COMPETITIVE OBEDIENCE
Border Collies and German Shepherds dominate this sport, but gundogs have also made their mark at the highest level. The Labrador has the intelligence to do well in competitive obedience; the challenge is producing the accuracy that is demanded. The classes start off being relatively easy and become progressively more challenging with additional exercises and the handler giving minimal instructions to the dog.

Exercises include:
• **Heelwork:** Dog and handler must complete a set pattern on and off the lead, which includes left turns, right turns, about turns, and changes of pace.
• **Recall:** This may be when the handler is stationary or moving.
• **Retrieve:** This may be a

dumbbell or any article chosen by the judge.
• **Sendaway:** The dog is sent to a designated spot and must go into an instant Down until he is recalled by the handler.
• **Stays:** The dog must stay in the Sit and in the Down for a set amount of time. In advanced classes, the hander is out of sight.
• **Scent:** The dog must retrieve a single cloth from a pre-arranged pattern of cloths that has his owner's scent, or, in advanced classes, the judge's scent. There may also be decoy cloths.
• **Distance control.** The dog must execute a series of moves (Sit, Stand, Down) without moving from his position and with the handler at a distance.
• **Agility.** In the US, agility is included with a retrieve over a jump, a long jump, and in directed jumping, where the dog must leave the handler and then, when instructed, clear the obstacle that is indicated.

Even though competitive

Labradors love agility, but you must ensure that your dog is fit and healthy enough to tackle the obstacles.

obedience requires accuracy and precision, make sure you make it fun for your Labrador, with lots of praise and rewards so that you motivate him to do his best. Many training clubs run advanced classes for those who want to compete in obedience, or you can hire the services of a professional trainer so you can have one-on-one sessions.

AGILITY
This fun sport has grown enormously in popularity over the past few years. If you fancy having a go, make sure you have good control over your Labrador and keep him slim. Agility is a very physical sport, which demands fitness from both dog and handler. A fat Lab is never going to make it as an agility competitor.

In agility competitions, each dog must complete a set course over a series of obstacles, which include:

• Jumps (upright hurdles and long jump)
• Weaves

• A-frame
• Dog walk
• Seesaw
• Tunnels (collapsible and rigid)
• Tyre

Dogs may compete in Jumping classes with jumps, tunnels and weaves, or in agility classes, which have the full set of equipment. Faults are awarded for poles down on the jumps, missed contact points on the A-frame, dog walk and seesaw, and refusals. If a dog takes the wrong course, he is eliminated. The winner is the dog that completes the course in the fastest time with no faults. As you progress up the levels, courses become progressively harder with more twists, turns and changes of direction.

If you want to get involved in agility, you will need to find a club that specialises in the sport (see Appendices). You will not be allowed to start training until your Labrador is 12 months old, and you cannot compete until he is 18 months old. This rule protects the dog, who may suffer injury if he

puts strain on bones and joints while he is still growing.

FIELD TRIALS
This is a sport where the Labrador excels, as it tests his natural working ability. There is now a split between working Labradors and show Labradors, and if you are interested in competing in field trials, you will need a Labrador that is bred from working lines.

In field trials, dogs are trained to work in an entirely natural environment. Nothing is set up, staged or artificial. The dogs may be asked to retrieve shot game from any type of terrain, including swamp, thick undergrowth and from water. They also need to perform blind retrieves, where they are sent out to find shot game when they haven't seen it fall. Dogs are judged on their natural game-finding abilities, their work in the shooting field, and their response to their handler. The two most crucial elements are steadiness and obedience.

Labradors are built for this

It takes hard work and skill to produce a top-class field trial competitor.

demanding job, with their waterproof coat, athletic physique and their great swimming ability. The other great plus factor is that Labs love to work closely with their handlers, so, if you put in the training, you could get to the top levels and even make your Labrador into a Field Trial Champion.

If you are not aiming for the dizzy heights of making up a Field Trial Champion, you can test your Labrador's working ability with the Gundog Working Certificate, which examines basic hunting and retrieving skills in the field. If a Show Champion gains a Gundog Working Certificate, he can become a full Champion.

WORKING TRIALS
This is a very challenging sport,

which is based on the civilian equivalent to police work. It has been introduced to the USA, but, at the present time, more emphasis is put on Tracking as a discipline in its own right. The Labrador, with his excellent sense of smell, excels as a tracking dog, and in the other components of Working Trials, which include:

• **Control:** Dog and handler must complete obedience exercises, but the work does not have to be as precise as it is in competitive obedience. In the advanced classes, manwork (where the dog works as a guard/protection dog) is a major feature.
• **Agility:** The dog must negotiate a 3 ft (0.91 m) hurdle, a 9 ft (2.75 m) long jump, and a 6 ft

(1.82 m) upright scale, which is the most taxing piece of dog equipment.
• **Nosework:** The dog must follow a track that has been laid over a set course. The surface may vary, and the length of time between the track being laid and the dog starting work is increased in the advanced classes.

The ladder of stakes are: Companion Dog, Utility Dog, Working Dog, Tracking Dog and Patrol Dog. In the US, tracking is a sport in its own right, and is very popular among Labrador owners.

If you want to get involved in working trials, you will need to find a specialist club or a trainer that specialises in training for working trials.

The Labrador is a talented dog and excels in many canine sports, but he is unbeatable in his role as a companion dog.

FLYBALL

Labradors are natural retrievers, so they can be easily trained to be flyball competitors. Flyball is a team sport; the dogs love it, and it is undoubtedly the noisiest of all the canine sports!

Four dogs are selected to run in a relay race against an opposing team. The dogs are sent out by their handlers to jump four hurdles, catch the ball from the flyball box, and then return over the hurdles. At the top level, this sport is fast and furious, and although it is dominated by Border Collies, reliable Labradors can make a big contribution. This is particularly true in multibreed competitions where the team is made up of four dogs of different breeds, and only one can be a Border Collie or a Working Sheepdog. Points are awarded to dogs and teams. Annual awards are given to top dogs and top teams, and milestone awards are given out to dogs as they attain points throughout their flyballing careers.

DANCING WITH DOGS

This sport is relatively new, but it is becoming increasingly popular. It is very entertaining to watch, but it is certainly not as simple as it looks. To perform a choreographed routine to music with your Labrador demands a huge amount of training.

Dancing with dogs is divided into two categories: Heelwork to Music and Canine Freestyle. In Heelwork to Music, the dog must work closely with his handler and show a variety of close 'heelwork' positions. In Canine Freestyle, the routine can be more flamboyant, with the dog working at a distance from the handler and performing spectacular tricks. Routines are judged on style and presentation, content and accuracy.

SUMMING UP

The Labrador is the most popular companion dog in the world, and deservedly so. He has an outstanding temperament, and he is fun and rewarding to live with. Make sure you keep your half of the bargain: spend time socialising and training your Labrador so that you can be proud to take him anywhere and he will always be a credit to you.

THE PERFECT LABRADOR

Chapter 7

Once dog showing started to become a popular hobby, it became necessary for every recognised breed to have a formulated, written description of the ideal specimen for that breed. Basically, this was a blueprint against which all competing dogs could be evaluated by judges in the show ring. Such blueprints are referred to as Breed Standards, and judges are obliged to judge dogs in the show ring against the relevant Standard for their breed. Breed Standards in the United Kingdom are controlled by the Kennel Club; in the United States the Breed Standards remain the property of the parent breed clubs, who maintain ultimate control.

The purpose of this chapter is to analyse the Labrador Breed Standard that applies to the United Kingdom (this Standard is in force in all countries affiliated with the Fédération Cynologique Internationale [FCI], as it adopts the Breed Standard from a breed's country of origin) and also the Breed Standard that is in force in the United States, and to examine any differences, however subtle, that may be present. First of all, we need to explore briefly the relative developments and context of both Breed Standards.

In 1916 the committee of the newly formed Labrador Retriever Club drew up the first British Breed Standard. The writers had the working abilities of the breed very much in their minds and

A judge should question whether the Labrador he sees in the ring is capable of carrying out the work he was originally bred to do.

The Labrador Retriever is a strongly-built, short-coupled dog.

they were at pains to clarify differences between the Labrador and its relatives, the Flat Coated Retriever and the Wavy Coated Retriever. The Standard remained unchanged until 1950, later revisions being made in 1982 and 1986.

The American Labrador Retriever Club Inc. was established in 1931. Initially, the US Standard was the same as the British one, but was later revised in the 1950s and was approved by the AKC in 1957, containing only a few differences to that of the home country. Later, amid controversy, a new Standard was composed and finally endorsed by the AKC in March 2004.

Nowadays, with the travel of show dogs between countries and continents being much easier and more frequent, it is all the more important to have a sound

knowledge and understanding of the requirements of different country's blueprints of the Labrador. Due to the slightly different headings under which the two Standards are written, the analysis has been conducted in a slightly rearranged order but all parts are still included.

Responding to public concern about the health of pure bred dogs, the KC has inserted the following introductory paragraph in all breed Standards:

A Breed Standard is the guideline which describes the ideal characteristics, temperament and appearance of a breed and ensures that the breed is fit for function. Absolute soundness is essential. Breeders and judges should at all times be careful to avoid obvious conditions or

exaggerations which would be detrimental in any way to the health, welfare or soundness of this breed. From time to time certain conditions or exaggerations may be considered to have the potential to affect dogs in some breeds adversely, and judges and breeders are requested to refer to the Kennel Club website for details of any such current issues. If a feature or quality is desirable it should only be present in the right measure.

GENERAL APPEARANCE
BRITISH
Strongly built, short-coupled, very active; broad in skull; broad and deep through chest and ribs; broad and strong over loins and hindquarters.

AKC
The Labrador Retriever is a strongly built, medium-sized, short-coupled dog possessing a sound, athletic, well-balanced conformation that enables it to function as a retrieving gun dog; the substance and soundness to hunt waterfowl or upland game for long hours under difficult conditions; the character and quality to win in the show ring; and the temperament to be a family companion. Physical features and mental characteristics should denote a dog bred to perform as an efficient Retriever of game with a stable temperament suitable for a variety of pursuits beyond the hunting environment. The most distinguishing characteristics of the Labrador Retriever are its short, dense,

weather resistant coat; an "otter" tail; a clean-cut head with broad back skull and moderate stop; powerful jaws; and its "kind," friendly eyes, expressing character, intelligence and good temperament.

Above all, a Labrador Retriever must be well balanced, enabling it to move in the show ring or work in the field with little or no effort. The typical Labrador possesses style and quality without over refinement, and substance without lumber or cloddiness. The Labrador is bred primarily as a working gun dog; structure and soundness are of great importance.

Right from the start, it is immediately apparent that the British Standard is much more concise and precise – the American Standard is lengthier to the point of being rather repetitive. However, its greater detail does give a certain depth of insight into the breed. For example, it refers to the breed's original function, to hunt and retrieve, from which the form of the dog derives. This background is assumed in the British Standard. Moreover, the American Standard makes it clear immediately that the breed's most distinguishing features are the head, coat and tail and draws attention to the need to avoid over-heavy, clumsy dogs, and stressing the need for sound conformation and movement. This can only be a good thing, as such exaggeration should be avoided like the plague! It is my

Intelligent, good-tempered and biddable: The hallmarks of good temperament.

belief that the Labrador should be a moderate breed, free from exaggeration (neither too fine nor too cloddy and cumbersome). I have certainly noticed a tendency, both in Britain and overseas when judging, that some people believe that bigger and heavier is best – in my opinion, it certainly is not!

CHARACTERISTICS AND TEMPERAMENT
BRITISH
Good-tempered, very agile, *which precludes excessive body weight or substance* (this last italicised statement recently added to KC Standard). Excellent nose, soft mouth; keen lover of water. Adaptable, devoted companion. Intelligent, keen and biddable, with a strong will to please. Kindly nature, with no trace of aggression or undue shyness.

AKC
True Labrador Retriever

temperament is as much a hallmark of the breed as the "otter" tail. The ideal disposition is one of a kindly, outgoing, tractable nature; eager to please and non-aggressive towards man or animal. The Labrador has much that appeals to people; his gentle ways, intelligence and adaptability make him an ideal dog. Aggressiveness towards humans or other animals, or any evidence of shyness in an adult should be severely penalized.

Here, although the American Standard is lengthier, the meaning of both is almost identical. There can be no doubt that the breed's specific temperament is one of the most important features that has made the breed so popular and indeed versatile. Correct breed temperament should be at the top of every breeder's list of priorities as, without it, a

Labrador is untypical. Whilst a degree of reticence may be acceptable in a youngster, a Labrador should never display aggression to either man or beast, and zero tolerance of aggression should be the order of the day, always.

The British Standard gives an important insight into the breed's working abilities, such as the need to have a soft mouth when retrieving game without injury and the breed's innate love of water. All owners of Labradors will be able to relate to this feature.

Whilst it is only a matter of semantics, the word 'agile' in the British Standard is rather puzzling. I often ask myself whether a dog that is "strongly built" and sturdy can be agile, as agile conjures up a picture of being nimble. What I feel is being stressed, and quite rightly so, is the need for this strongly built dog to avoid exaggeration so that it is still athletic and fit for the purpose for which it was originally bred.

HEAD AND SKULL: EYES, EARS AND MOUTH
BRITISH
CRANIAL REGION
Skull: Broad. Clean-cut without fleshy cheeks.
Stop: Defined.
FACIAL REGION:
Nose: Wide, nostrils well developed.
Muzzle: Powerful, not snipey.
Jaws/teeth: Jaws of medium length, jaws and teeth strong with a perfect, regular and complete scissor bite, i.e. upper teeth closely overlapping lower teeth and set square to the jaws.
Eyes: Medium size, expressing intelligence and good temper; brown or hazel.
Ears: Not large or heavy, hanging close to head and set rather far back.

AKC
Skull: The skull should be wide; well developed but without exaggeration. The skull and foreface should be on parallel planes and of approximately equal length. There should be a moderate stop – the brow slightly pronounced so that the skull is not absolutely in a straight line with the nose. The brow ridges aid in defining the stop. The head should be clean-cut and free from fleshy cheeks; the bony structure of the skull chiseled beneath the eye with no prominence in the cheek. The skull may show some median line; the occipital bone is not conspicuous in mature dogs. Lips should not be squared off or pendulous, but fall away in a curve toward the throat. A wedge-shape head, or a head long and narrow in muzzle and back skull is incorrect as are massive, cheeky heads. The jaws are powerful and free from snippiness – the muzzle neither long and narrow nor short and stubby.
Nose: The nose should be wide and the nostrils well-developed. The nose should be black on black or yellow dogs, and brown on chocolates. Nose

The skull is wide and well developed, but without exaggeration.

colour fading to a lighter shade is not a fault. A thoroughly pink nose or one lacking in any pigment is a disqualification.

Teeth: The teeth should be strong and regular with a scissors bite; the lower teeth just behind, but touching the inner side of the upper incisors. A level bite is acceptable, but not desirable. Undershot, overshot, or misaligned teeth are serious faults. Full dentition is preferred. Missing molars or pre-molars are serious faults.

Ears: The ears should hang moderately close to the head, set rather far back, and somewhat low on the skull; slightly above eye level. Ears should not be large and heavy, but in proportion with the skull and reach to the inside of the eye when pulled forward.

Eyes: Kind, friendly eyes imparting good temperament, intelligence and alertness are a hallmark of the breed. They should be of medium size, set well apart, and neither protruding nor deep set. Eye colour should be brown in black and yellow Labradors, and brown or hazel in chocolates. Black, or yellow eyes give a harsh expression and are undesirable. Small eyes, set close together or round prominent eyes are not typical of the breed. Eye rims are black in black and yellow Labradors; and brown in chocolates. Eye

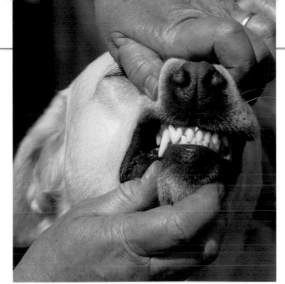

The teeth should meet in a scissor bite, with the teeth on the upper jaw closely overlapping the teeth on the lower jaw.

rims without pigmentation is a disqualification.

The head is an extremely important feature of the Labrador for if you were to choose just one feature to distinguish the breed, you would surely choose the head. Indeed, the correct head and expression are two of the most important features of the breed that constitute breed type – this means that a Labrador should look like a Labrador and no other breed.

As described in both Standards, the head should be free from fleshy cheeks and the muzzle must be of a length conducive to carrying game, therefore any resemblance to a head akin to a Rottweiler is alien to the breed and must be avoided. Similarly, some of the heads on the working dogs are too fine and snipey, or too flat in the stop, with peculiarly, high-set ears, which is also foreign. Both Standards refer to the need to have a wide nose

and well-developed nostrils, obviously in order to help the Labrador's scenting ability and utility in the field.

The details given to the eye in the AKC Standard are more detailed than the British one, but it is interesting to note that the hazel eye is unacceptable to the AKC apart from in chocolates. Similarly, the AKC Standard requirement of black eye rims on yellows is peculiar too. What I believe should be written is dark instead of black. The two most important points to remember are that, firstly, the eyes should never too black or too light – the overly dark, black eye gives a blank, untypical expression and the overly light eye gives a staring, hard expression, also undesirable. Secondly, dark pigmentation is required and 'yellow livers' (e.g. yellows lacking pigmentation), which is most unattractive, should be avoided at all costs. Arthur and Peggy Kelley (Bradking), who are the only breeders in the UK to have bred a Champion in all three colours and from whom I purchased my first title holder, instilled in me that the dark brown pigmentation in chocolates should be evident not only around the eye rims but should also be discernable inside the cheeks. The Bradking chocolates were certainly renowned for their excellent pigmentation and eye colour.

Both Standards in effect say similar things on ears, bearing in mind that high-set ears give the

The body is short-coupled with a level topline.

Labrador an untypical, almost terrier-like look. The ears should have no indication of being large or heavy in any way and should be set far back. Labradors that 'fly' their ears (e.g. pin them back) give a less desirable expression and what is clear in both Standards is that the expression of the dog denotes its temperament and outlook on life.

NECK, TOPLINE AND BODY
BRITISH
NECK: Clean, strong, powerful, set into well placed shoulders.

BODY
Back: Level topline.
Loins: Wide, short-coupled and strong.
Chest: Of good width and depth, with well sprung barrel ribs – *this effect not to be produced by carrying excessive weight* (this italicised statement recently added to the KC Standard).

AKC
Neck: The neck should be of proper length to allow the dog to retrieve game easily. It should be muscular and free from throatiness. The neck should rise strongly from the shoulders with a moderate arch. A short, thick neck or a "ewe" neck is incorrect.
Topline: The back is strong and the topline is level from the withers to the croup when standing or moving. However, the loin should show evidence of flexibility for athletic endeavour.
Body: The Labrador should be short-coupled, with good spring of ribs tapering to a moderately wide chest. The Labrador should not be narrow chested; giving the appearance of hollowness between the front legs, nor should it have a wide spreading, Bulldog-like front. Correct chest conformation will result in tapering between the

front legs that allows unrestricted forelimb movement. Chest breadth that is either too wide or too narrow for efficient movement and stamina is incorrect. Slab-sided individuals are not typical of the breed; equally objectionable are rotund or barrel chested specimens. The underline is almost straight, with little or no tuck-up in mature animals. Loins should be short, wide and strong; extending to well-developed, powerful hindquarters. When viewed from the side, the Labrador Retriever shows a well-developed, but not exaggerated forechest.

The meaning within both Standards is that the neck of the Labrador should not be long – rather it needs to be clean and strong. With an animal that has an overly long neck, the strength will be reduced and it is necessary for the function of the dog that it has a strong neck with which it can easily pick up game once it has fallen to the ground. A Labrador with the correct neck and forequarters assembly (discussed in the next paragraph) will have a look of beauty and quality about it.

The backline of the dog needs to be level; one of the ugliest features of an untypical backline is when the tail-set is low and the topline slopes away at the croup area. Also, backlines that have a dip either behind the withers or further along the backline are to be avoided and show a weakness that is a serious fault.

Both Standards refer to the requirement of a short-coupled

Pictured at seven months of age, this is a very promising youngster, but lacking the substance of a mature dog.

Now five years old and a Champion, fulfilling all his early promise.

body. This must not be confused with being 'short backed' – the correct body is one that has a long ribcage and a short, strong loin, which gives strength and power. An animal can be short backed with a very short ribcage and quite long loin – this is not typical; rather the body should be more of a rectangle, rather than a square, with the ribs extending well back and the loin being short. Whilst it depends on the size of one's hand, the loin should be approximately the length of a hand's breadth.

The two Standards differ quite remarkably in a couple of areas in this section. The British Standard mentions that the ribs should be the shape of a barrel whilst the AKC standard mentions that 'rotund or barrel chested specimens' are 'equally objectionable'. It is the opinion of this author that the ribs should be barrel shaped, as this is conducive to plenty of heart and lung room, which is needed of a functional working animal. With the barrel rib comes the breadth of chest as required by both Standards – this

is necessary for strength, heart and lung room and for performing the task for which the breed was originally intended.

Moreover, the AKC Standard refers to the underline being 'almost straight with little or no tuck-up'. Although this is not mentioned in the British Standard, it is the opinion of this particular writer that the AKC requirement is most concerning. The underline should not be tucked up in any way like that seen in the Whippet breed; however, an underline that is almost straight lends itself to

The forequarters should be muscular and balanced with the hindquarters.

Too much bone is as undesirable as too little bone, and short legged, heavy-boned individuals are not typical of the breed. Viewed from the side, the elbows should be directly under the withers, and the front legs should be perpendicular to the ground and well under the body. The elbows should be close to the ribs without looseness. Tied-in elbows or being "out at the elbows" interfere with free movement and are serious faults. Pasterns should be strong and short and should slope slightly from the perpendicular line of the leg. Feet are strong and compact, with well-arched toes and well-developed pads. Dew claws may be removed. Splayed feet, hare feet, knuckling over, or feet turning in or out are serious faults.

The forequarters of any animal (canine or equine) are extremely important, as the assembly of the forequarters determines the whole balance of the animal. It is a commonly held belief among breed enthusiasts on both sides of the Atlantic that one of the most commonly seen faults in the breed is incorrect front assembly. This can result from insufficient length and layback of the shoulder blades and/or short, steep upper arms. An incorrect front can still be produced with a long and sloping shoulder if the upperarm is too short and straight. Reference to the upperarm is omitted in the British Standard and details of the classic and desired angulation with regard to the upperarm forming an angle of 90 degrees with the shoulder in

the untypical appearance of an animal that is level in the belly or otherwise badly overweight, out of condition or in whelp. This is certainly not typical of the Labrador.

FOREQUARTERS
BRITISH
Shoulders long and sloping. Forelegs well boned and straight from elbow to ground when viewed from either front or side.

AKC
Forequarters should be muscular, well coordinated and balanced with the hindquarters.

Shoulders: The shoulders are well laid-back, long and sloping, forming an angle with the upper arm of approximately 90 degrees that permits the dog to move his forelegs in an easy manner with strong forward reach. Ideally, the length of the shoulder blade should equal the length of the upper arm. Straight shoulder blades, short upper arms or heavily muscled or loaded shoulders, all restricting free movement, are incorrect.
Front legs: When viewed from the front, the legs should be straight with good strong bone.

The judge looks at the Labrador to get an overall impression.

The hands-on examination starting from the front...

...and working through to the rear.

The exhibitor gets the dog's attention so he looks alert, leaving the judge with a good impression.

the AKC Standard may seem rather complicated to the uninitiated. What is important to remember is that when you stand back and look at a dog, the line from behind the head down the neck to the point of the withers should be longer than the line from the throat to the forechest if the forequarters angulation is correct. Similarly, if the dog has correct front angulation, on the move it will have a good reach of stride that covers the ground as opposed to a rather choppy, shorter-stepping action, which is uneconomical and useless in a working dog.

While the legs should be well boned, as required in the British Standard, it is my opinion that we often see Labradors with too much bone, particularly in the show ring. Therefore, I like the detail and further clarification in the AKC Standard with regard to this area. The bone should be of good quality, e.g. round bone that does not taper away too much to the pasterns; however, the bone should not be so heavy as to impede movement, resulting in a heavy, ponderous action seen in some specimens.

FEET
BRITISH
Round, compact; well arched toes and well developed pads.

AKC
Feet are strong and compact with well arched toes and well developed pads. Dew claws may be removed. Splay feet, hare feet, knuckling over or feet turning in or out are serious faults.

The hindquarters are the powerhouse of the Labrador.

The feet are a most important feature of the Labrador. The AKC Standard draws attention to the serious fault of 'knuckling over', which results from pasterns that are very upright and which make bad shock absorbers when the dog is either on the move or landing on the ground after a jump. In the British Standard, it is implied by the fact that the forelegs should be straight from the elbow to the ground that knuckling over is undesirable. What is important to remember is that the pasterns should be ever so slightly sloping in order to have a degree of spring and 'give'.

HINDQUARTERS
BRITISH
Well developed, not sloping to tail; well turned stifle. Hocks well let down, cow hocks highly undesirable.

AKC
The Labrador's hindquarters are broad, muscular and well developed from the hip to the hock with well-turned stifles and strong short hocks. Viewed from the rear, the hind legs are straight and parallel. Viewed from the side, the angulation of the rear legs is in balance with the front. The hind legs are strongly boned, muscled with moderate angulation at the stifle, and powerful, clearly defined thighs. The stifle is strong and there is no slippage of the patellae while in motion or when standing. The hock joints are strong, well let down and do not slip or hyper-extend while in motion or when standing. Angulation of both stifle and hock joint is such as to achieve the optimal balance of drive and traction. When standing the rear toes are only

slightly behind the point of the rump. Over angulation produces a sloping topline not typical of the breed. Feet are strong and compact, with well-arched toes and well-developed pads. Cow-hocks, spread hocks, sickle hocks and over-angulation are serious structural defects and are to be faulted.

The hindquarters are the 'power house' of the dog, which gives it the strength to drive forwards with some strength. This can only be achieved with correct angulation of the hindquarters and it is interesting to note that the British Standard draws attention to the connection with the topline, e.g. that there should be no falling away at the croup. It is imperative to note that hocks which are well let down (remember that the hock is a joint) nearly always accompany good hindquarters. Generally speaking, the hindquarters of dogs seen in the show ring today are more developed than in past years – a glance at the photographs of animals from the 1950s and 1960s reveals that they had slightly less hind angulation. One must remember, however, that although there should be width of thigh, over-angulation should be avoided and is indeed a weakness. For example, it can lead to a sloping topline, which is undesirable, or excessive angulation can lead to cow hocks, which are highly undesirable in both AKC and British Standards. Cow hocks, which sometimes accompany overangulated hindquarters, are a severe weakness and make it impossible for the dog to show any drive when moving from behind. No reference is made in the UK Standard to slipping patellae as in the AKC Standard, but such anatomical defects, perhaps more common in some other breeds of dogs than Labradors, is a serious weakness.

TAIL
BRITISH
Distinctive feature, very thick towards the base, gradually tapering towards tip, medium length, free from feathering, but clothed thickly all round with short, thick, dense coat, thus giving rounded appearance described as "Otter" tail. May be carried gaily, but should not curl over back.

AKC
The tail is a distinguishing feature of the breed. It should be very thick at the base, gradually tapering toward the tip, of medium length, and extending no longer than to the hock. The tail should be free from feathering and clothed thickly all around with the Labrador's short, dense coat, thus having that peculiar rounded appearance that has been described as the "otter" tail. The tail should follow the

The judge will ask the handler to move the dog so he can assess movement from the front, the rear, and from the side.

topline in repose or when in motion. It may be carried gaily, but should not curl over the back. Extremely short tails or long thin tails are serious faults. The tail completes the balance of the Labrador by giving it a flowing line from the top of the head to the tip of the tail. Docking or otherwise altering the length or natural carriage of the tail is a disqualification.

Both Standards explain exactly what is required here. The "otter" tail is one that, once seen, is never forgotten and is always accompanied by a typical coat. Without being clothed in the typical Labrador coat, the rounded appearance and feather-free "otter" tail will never be achieved. Just as with all of the other features of a true Labrador, the otter-like tail does serve a purpose and is intrinsically connected to the breed's function and origins. The tail adds greatly to the dog's ability to swim competently in water, as it acts as a rudder.

As regards the tail carriage, it is only the interpretation of this writer, but one must remember that both Standards state that the tail "may" be carried gaily. To me, this does not infer that it should be, but that it is not a fault should it be carried gaily as long as it does not curl over the back. On the subject of tail carriage, it is my opinion that the dog's tail carriage is often indicative of the dog's nature, temperament and biddability. Nothing looks better than a Labrador with a true, otter-like tail, carried straight off the back whilst in motion or seen gently wagging whilst in repose.

MOVEMENT
BRITISH
Free, covering adequate ground; straight and true in front and rear.

AKC
Movement of the Labrador Retriever should be free and effortless. When watching a dog move toward oneself, there should be no sign of elbows out. Rather, the elbows should be held neatly to the body with the legs not too close together. Moving straight forward without pacing or weaving, the legs should form straight lines, with all parts moving in the same plane. Upon viewing the dog from the rear, one should have the impression that the hind legs move as nearly as possible in a parallel line with the front legs. The hocks should do their full share of the work, flexing well, giving the appearance of power and strength. When viewed from the side, the shoulders should move freely and effortlessly, and the foreleg should reach forward close to the ground with extension. A short, choppy movement or high knee action indicates a straight shoulder; paddling indicates long, weak pasterns; and a short, stilted rear gait indicates a straight rear assembly; all are serious faults. Movement faults interfering with performance including weaving; side-winding; crossing over; high knee action; paddling; and short, choppy movement, should be severely penalized.

While I have no real complaints with the very concise British

Standard, the AKC Standard does give more insight for the uninitiated into what is required by correct movement. I believe that it is on the move that the whole animal and its working parts can be seen at their best and are most revealing. In the show ring, I believe that more judges need to evaluate the dogs when in motion, as it is only then that the whole balance of the dog can be seen. Correct movement needs to be neither too wide nor too close behind and in profile needs to show reach in front and drive from behind, resulting from correct and balanced angulation both fore and aft. In short, the movement should be effortless – any action that does not appear to be without effort is incorrect.

My one criticism of the British Standard is in the use of the word "adequate" in the movement clause. This word is a term of mediocrity, which to me has the inference of being only just enough. Surely a dog with the origins and function of a Labrador and which is a "very active" dog, should show more than merely "adequate" ground coverage? I would therefore prefer the words "adequate ground" to be replaced with the word "plenty of ground".

COAT
BRITISH
Distinctive feature, short, dense, without wave or feathering, giving fairly hard feel to the touch; weather-resistant undercoat.

AKC
The coat is a distinctive feature of the Labrador Retriever. It

The yellow Labrador's coat can range from light cream to red fox.

should be short, straight and very dense, giving a fairly hard feeling to the hand. The Labrador should have a soft, weather-resistant undercoat that provides protection from water, cold and all types of ground cover. A slight wave down the back is permissible. Woolly coats, soft silky coats, and sparse slick coats are not typical of the breed, and should be severely penalized.

Just as with the head, the coat is such a distinguishing feature of the breed that it denotes breed type. The coat, which needs to be a double coat, with a fairly hard topcoat to the touch, covering a thick, weather-resisting undercoat, is essential in the breed, considering once again its origins and function as a waterdog. The coat is essential in keeping the dog well protected against freezing-cold waters – dogs with the true coat come out of water, have a quick shake and the water is repelled, never getting anywhere near their skin. Only if a Labrador has the correct double coat will the typical otter-like tail, which is free from feathering, result.

In the AKC Standard it draws attention to a slight wave in the coat along the back being allowed. Several eminently successful and knowledgeable UK breeders would never penalise a coat that has a topcoat with a slight wave, but the watchword here is "slight".

COLOUR
BRITISH
Wholly black, yellow or liver/chocolate. Yellows range from light cream to red fox. Small white spot on chest permissible.

AKC
The Labrador Retriever coat colours are black, yellow and chocolate. Any other colour or a combination of colours is a disqualification. A small white spot on the chest is permissible, but not desirable. White hairs from aging or scarring are not to be misinterpreted as brindling. Black: Blacks are all black. A black with brindle markings or a black with tan markings is a disqualification. Yellow: Yellows may range in colour from fox-red to light cream, with variations in shading on the ears, back, and underparts of the dog. Chocolate: Chocolates can vary in shade from light to dark chocolate. Chocolate with brindle or tan markings is a disqualification.

Here, once again, the AKC Standard goes into more detail than its British counterpart. What is important to remember is that whether the Labrador is black, yellow or chocolate, the colour should be wholly that colour and the term 'yellow' covers all shades of the colour from cream to red fox. How often do you erroneously

The American Standard allows for chocolates to vary in shade from light to dark – but in the UK, a dark chocolate is preferred.

hear people refer to a Labrador as being "golden"? Furthermore, the use of the word "wholly" negates the need to mention the mismarking that brindling represents.

Neither Standard mentions that sometimes, often accompanying a really good, typical, double coat can come an undercoat that has white hairs in it. Similarly, sometimes there can be a white ring at the base of the hair one-third of the way down the tail, which again often accompanies a perfectly typical and correct Labrador coat.

SIZE, PROPORTION AND SUBSTANCE
BRITISH
Ideal height at withers: Dogs 56-57 cm (22-22.5 in); bitches: 55-56 cm (21.5-22 in).

AKC
Size: **The height at the withers for a dog is 22.5 to 24.5 inches; for a bitch is 21.5 to 23.5 inches. Any variance greater than half an inch above or below these heights is a disqualification. Approximate weight of dogs and bitches in working condition: dogs 65 to 80 pounds; bitches 55 to 70 pounds.**
The minimum height ranges set forth in the paragraph above shall not apply to dogs or bitches under twelve months of age.
Proportion: **Short-coupled; length from the point of the shoulder to the point of the rump is equal to or slightly longer than the distance from the withers to the ground. Distance from the elbow to the ground should be equal to one**

half of the height at the withers. **The brisket should extend to the elbows, but not perceptibly deeper. The body must be of sufficient length to permit a straight, free and efficient stride; but the dog should never appear low and long or tall and leggy in outline.**
Substance: **Substance and bone proportionate to the overall dog. Light, "weedy" individuals are definitely incorrect; equally objectionable are cloddy lumbering specimens. Labrador Retrievers shall be shown in working condition well-muscled and without excess fat.**

With regard to height, there is a difference between the UK and AKC Standards – the latter allows for bigger dogs and bitches. I much prefer the British Standard in this respect, which, in referring to the height, mentions the word "ideal". This allows a degree of manoeuvrability either side of the desire height norm, which I believe to be much preferable to the AKC Standard which, should the "wicket" be called and the dog fall half an inch either side of the height limits, it can be disqualified. The use of the word "ideal" allows common sense to prevail – what is most important is that regardless of the dog's precise height at the withers, it is well balanced and that the dog as a whole is viewed and judged.

FAULTS AND DISQUALIFICATIONS
BRITISH
Any departure from the foregoing points should be considered a fault and the

seriousness with which the fault should be regarded should be in exact proportion to its degree and its effect upon the health and welfare of the dog.

AKC
Disqualifications:

1. Any deviation from the height prescribed in the Standard.
2. A thoroughly pink nose or one lacking in any pigment.
3. Eye rims without pigment.
4. Docking or otherwise altering the length or natural carriage of the tail.
5. Any other colour or a combination of colours other than black, yellow or chocolate as described in the Standard.

The clause from the British Standard covers all aspects of deviance from the Standard, allowing personal interpretation to prevail while still paying particular attention to the health and well-being of the dog. I am surprised that the AKC Standard makes no mention of entirety in male animals.

SUMMARY

In reality, there is no such thing as the perfect Labrador – it is rather akin to the search for the Holy Grail whereby the quest and search for an animal as close as possible to the Breed Standard is something that breeders the world over are trying to achieve.

A comparison of the American and British/FCI Standards for the Labrador Retriever differ in several respects, although the overall picture and message is, I would suggest, very much the same. Whereas the British/FCI Standard is concise and in some respects brief, it nevertheless succeeds in detailing what is required in the Labrador Retriever. Obviously, I am more familiar with this Standard and feel that it is excellent. The only aspect that I would like to see altered is the section on movement. Here, I feel it should call for more than the dog covering adequate ground on the move. Surely an athletic, very active dog like the Labrador Retriever should be able to demonstrate good ground coverage on the move, at least.

The American Breed Standard goes into much greater detail in some respects and certain aspects are definitely different, for example the size requirements. However, just like the British/FCI Standard, opinion is still a matter of interpretation, and is bound to be subjective. What no Standard can do is differentiate between excellence, good quality, and mediocrity – that is something that a judge and breeder must do for themselves, with a blueprint of the Breed Standard firmly fixed in their mind as an ideal to which to aspire.

It is the judge's job to assess each dog on its merits. The Labradors that conform most closely to the Breed Standard will be placed.

HAPPY AND HEALTHY

Chapter 8

The Labrador Retriever is a generally resilient, active dog, developed as a gundog with a good life-span running into double figures, provided his needs are met. He is as well suited to being trained to the gun, living in a kennel and waiting patiently at his master's feet for the command to retrieve game as he is to being a loyal member of the family.

The Labrador is renowned as a faithful companion, a willing friend on a non-conditional basis. He will, however, of necessity rely on you for food and shelter, accident prevention and medication. A healthy Labrador is a tail-wagging, happy dog, looking to please his owner. Many will spontaneously hunt out an item such as a favourite ball or a slipper to give to their owner when they walk in the door, to welcome them home.

There are a few genetic conditions that occur in the Labrador, such as hip dysplasia and hereditary cataracts, which will be covered in depth later in the chapter.

A major omission in the Labrador's design plan was a conscience when it comes to food. This is a breed notorious for greed – there is no doubt that his head is ruled by his stomach! Those lovely dark brown eyes can be so expressive and persuasive. His brain has no concept of weight control. My own Labrador was once caught with her head in the food bin when the lid had been inadvertently left off!

ROUTINE HEALTH CARE

VACCINATION

There is much debate over the issue of vaccination at the moment. Timing of the final part of the initial vaccination course for a puppy and the frequency of subsequent booster vaccinations are both under scrutiny. An evaluation of the relative risk for each disease plays a part, depending on the local situation. Many owners think that the actual vaccination is the protection, so that their puppy can go out for walks as soon as he or she has had the final part of the puppy vaccination course. This is not the case.

The rationale behind vaccination is to stimulate the immune system into producing protective antibodies that will be triggered if the patient is subsequently exposed to that particular disease. This means that a further one or two weeks will have to pass before an effective level of protection will have developed.

Vaccines against viruses stimulate longer-lasting protection than those against bacteria, whose effect may only persist for a matter of months in some cases. There is also the possibility of an

Initially the puppies will receive immunity from their mother's milk.

A course of vaccinations is generally started when a puppy leaves the litter and is in his new home.

individual failing to mount a full immune response to a vaccination: although the vaccine schedule may have been followed as recommended, that particular dog remains vulnerable.

An individual's level of protection against rabies, as demonstrated by the antibody titre in a blood sample, is routinely tested in the UK in order to fulfil the requirements of the Pet Travel Scheme (PETS). This is not the case with other individual diseases in order to gauge the need for booster vaccination or to determine the effect of a course of vaccines; instead, your veterinary surgeon will advise a protocol based upon the vaccines available, local disease prevalence, and the

lifestyle of you and your dog.

It is worth remembering that maintaining a fully effective level of immune protection against the disease appropriate to your locale is vital: these are serious diseases that may result in the demise of your dog, and some may have the potential to be passed on to his human family (so-called zoonotic potential for transmission). This is where you will be grateful for your veterinary surgeon's own knowledge and advice.

The American Animal Hospital Association laid down guidance at the end of 2006 for the vaccination of dogs in North America. Core diseases were defined as distemper, adenovirus, parvovirus and rabies. So-called

non-core diseases are kennel cough, Lyme disease and leptospirosis; a decision to vaccinate against one or more non-core diseases will be based on an individual's level of risk, determined on lifestyle and where you live in the US.

Do remember, however, that the booster visit to the veterinary surgery is not 'just' for a booster. I am regularly correcting my clients when they announce that they have 'just' brought their pet for a booster. Instead, this appointment is a chance for a full health check and evaluation of how a particular dog is doing. After all, we are all conversant with the adage that a human year is equivalent to seven canine years. There have been attempts in recent times to reset the scale for two reasons: small breeds live longer than giant breeds, and dogs are living longer than previously. I have seen dogs of 17 and 18 years of age, but to say a dog is 119 or 126 years old is plainly meaningless. It does emphasise the fact, though, that a dog's health can change dramatically over the course of a single year because dogs age at a far greater rate than humans.

For me as a veterinary surgeon, the booster vaccination visit is a challenge: how much can I find of which the owner was unaware, such as rotten teeth or a heart murmur? Even monitoring bodyweight year upon year is of use because bodyweight can creep up, or down, without an owner realising. Being overweight is unhealthy, but it may take an outsider's remark to make an owner realise that there is a problem. Conversely, a drop in bodyweight may be the only pointer to an underlying problem.

The diseases against which dogs are vaccinated include:

ADENOVIRUS
Canine Adenovirus 1 (CAV-1) affects the liver (hepatitis) and the classic 'blue eye' appearance in some affected dogs, whilst CAV-2 is a cause of kennel cough (see later). Vaccines often include both canine adenoviruses.

The vet can give your Labrador a thorough check-up when he has his booster injection.

DISTEMPER
This disease is also called 'hardpad' from the characteristic changes to the pads of the paws. It has a worldwide distribution, but fortunately vaccination has been very effective at reducing its occurrence. It is caused by a virus and affects the respiratory, gastro-intestinal (gut) and nervous systems, so it causes a wide range of illnesses. Fox and urban stray dog populations are most at risk, and therefore responsible for local outbreaks.

KENNEL COUGH
This is also known as infectious tracheobronchitis – Bordetella bronchiseptica is not only a major cause of kennel cough but also a common secondary infection on top of another cause. Being a

bacterium, it is susceptible to treatment with appropriate antibiotics, but the immunity stimulated by the vaccine is therefore short-lived (six to 12 months).

This vaccine is often in a form to be administered down the nostrils in order to stimulate local immunity at the point of entry, so to speak. Do not be alarmed to see your veterinary surgeon using a needle and syringe to draw up the vaccine, because the needle will be replaced with a special plastic introducer, allowing the vaccine to be gently instilled into each nostril. Dog generally resent being held more than the actual intra nasal vaccine, and I have learnt that covering the patient's eyes helps greatly.

Kennel cough is, however, rather a catch-all term for any cough spreading within a dog population not just in kennels but also between dogs at a training session or breed show, or even mixing in the park. Many of these infections may not be B. bronchiseptica but other viruses, for which one can only treat symptomatically. Parainfluenza virus is often included in a vaccine programme because it is a common viral cause of kennel cough.

Kennel cough can seem alarming. There is a persistent cough accompanied by white

Kennel cough is highly infectious and will spread rapidly among dogs that are in close contact.

frothy spittle, which can last for a matter of weeks, during which time the patient is highly infectious to other dogs. I remember when it ran through our five Border Collies – there were white patches of froth on the floor wherever you looked! Other features include sneezing, a runny nose, and eyes sore with conjunctivitis. Fortunately, these infections are generally self-limiting, most dogs recovering without any long-lasting problems, but an elderly dog may be knocked sideways by it, akin to the effects of a common cold on a frail, elderly person.

LEPTOSPIROSIS
Contact with rats and their urine is the common way that dogs contract this disease, also known as Weil's disease in humans. This is a zoonotic disease with implications for all those in contact with an affected dog.

The UK National Rodent Survey 2003 found a wild brown rat population of 60 million, equivalent at the time to one rat per person. I have heard it said that, in the UK, you are never more than a foot (30 cm) from a rat! This means that there is as much a risk for the Labrador living with a family on the edge of a town as the working Labrador retrieving game from ditches, ponds and farmland.

The situation in the US is less clear cut. Blanket vaccination against leptospirosis is not considered necessary, as it only occurs in certain areas, so you must be guided by your veterinarian.

LYME DISEASE
This is a bacterial infection transmitted by hard ticks. It is therefore found in those specific areas of the US where ticks are found, such as north-eastern states, some southern states, California and the upper Mississippi region. It does also occur in the UK but at a low level,

so vaccination is not routinely offered.

Clinical disease is manifested primarily as limping due to arthritis, but other organs affected include the heart, kidneys and nervous system. It is readily treatable with appropriate antibiotics, once diagnosed, but the causal bacterium, Borrelia burgdorferi, is not cleared from the body totally and will persist.

Prevention requires both vaccination and tick control, especially as there are other diseases transmitted by ticks. Ticks carrying B. burgdorferi will transmit it to humans as well, but an infected dog cannot pass it to a human.

PARVOVIRUS
This appeared in the late 1970s, when it was thought that the UK's dog population would be decimated by it. This notion terrified me at the time but fortunately it did not happen on the scale envisaged. Occurrence is mainly low now, thanks to vaccination. It is also occasionally seen in the elderly unvaccinated dog.

RABIES
This is another zoonotic disease and there are very strict control measures in place. Vaccines were once only available in the UK on an individual basis for dogs being taken abroad. Pets travelling into the UK had to serve six months' compulsory quarantine so that any pet incubating rabies would be identified before release back into the general population. Under the Pet Travel Scheme, provided certain criteria are met

(visit the DEFRA website for up-to-date information – www.defra.gov.uk) then dogs can re-enter the UK without being quarantined.

Dogs to be imported into the US have to show that they were vaccinated against rabies at least 30 days previously; otherwise, they have to serve effective internal quarantine for 30 days from the date of vaccination against rabies, in order to ensure they are not incubating rabies. The exception is dogs entering from countries recognised as being rabies-free, in which case it has to be proved that they lived in that country for at least six months beforehand.

PARASITES

A parasite is defined as an organism deriving benefit on a one-way basis from another, the host. It goes without saying that it is not to the parasite's advantage to harm the host to such an extent that the benefit is lost, especially if it results in the death of the host.

This means a dog could harbour parasites, internal and/or external, without there being any signs apparent to the owner.

Many canine parasites can, however, transfer to humans with variable consequences, so routine preventative treatment is advised against particular parasites. Just as

The breeder will start a worming programme, which you will need to continue.

with vaccination, risk assessment plays a part – for example, there is no need for routine heartworm treatment in the UK (at present), but it is vital in the US and in Mediterranean countries.

INTERNAL PARASITES

Roundworms (nematodes): These are the spaghetti-like worms that you may have been unfortunate enough to have seen passed in faeces or brought up in vomit. Most of the de-worming treatments in use today cause the adult roundworms to disintegrate, thankfully, so that treating puppies in particular is not as unpleasant as it used to be!

Most puppies will have a worm burden, mainly of a particular roundworm species (Toxocara canis), which reactivates within the dam's tissues during pregnancy and passes to the foetuses developing in the womb. It is therefore important to treat the dam both during and after pregnancy, as well as the puppies.

Professional advice is to continue worming every month. There are roundworm eggs in the environment and, unless you examine your dog's faeces under a microscope on a very regular basis for the presence of roundworm eggs, you will be unaware of your dog having picked up roundworms, unless he should have such a heavy burden that he passes the adults.

It takes a few weeks from the time that a dog swallows a Toxocara canis roundworm egg to himself passing viable eggs (the pre-patent period). There are de-worming products that are active all the time, which will provide continuous protection when administered as often as directed. Otherwise, treating every month will, in effect, cut in before a dog could theoretically become a source of roundworm eggs to the general population.

It is the risk to human health that is so important: T. canis roundworms will migrate within our tissues and can cause all manner of problems, not least of which is blindness. If a dog has roundworms, the eggs also find their way on to his coat where they can be picked up during stroking and cuddling.

You should always carefully pick up your dog's faeces and dispose of them appropriately, which will not only reduce the chance for environmental contamination with all manner of infections but also make walking more pleasant underfoot.

Tapeworms (cestodes): When considering the general dog population, the primary source of the commonest tapeworm species will be fleas, which can carry the eggs. Most multi-wormers will be active against these tapeworms, not because they are a hazard to human health but because it is unpleasant to see the wriggly 'rice grain' tapeworm segments emerging from your dog's back

passage while he is lying in front of the fire, and usually when you have had guests for dinner!

There are specific requirements for treatment with praziquantel within 24 to 48 hours of return into the UK under the PETS. This is to prevent the inadvertent introduction of Echinococcus multilocularis, a tapeworm carried by foxes on mainland Europe, which is transmissible to humans, causing serious or even fatal liver disease.

Heartworm (Dirofilaria immitis): Heartworm infection has been diagnosed in dogs all over the world. There are two prerequisites: presence of mosquitoes and a warm, humid climate.

When a female mosquito bites an infected animal, it acquires D. immitis in its circulating form, as microfilariae. A warm environmental temperature is

needed for these microfilariae to develop into the infective third-stage larvae (L3) within the mosquitoes, the so-called intermediate host. L3 larvae are then transmitted by the mosquito when it next bites a dog. Therefore, while heartworm infection is found in all the states of the US, it is at differing levels such that an occurrence in Alaska, for example, is probably a reflection of a visiting dog having previously picked up the infection elsewhere.

Heartworm infection is not currently a problem in the UK, except for those dogs contracting it while abroad without suitable preventative treatment. Global warming and its effect on the UK's climate, however, could change that.

It is a potentially life-threatening condition, with dogs of all breeds and ages being susceptible without preventative treatment. The larvae can grow to 14 inches (35.5 cm) within the right side of the heart, causing primarily signs of heart failure and ultimately liver and kidney damage. It can be treated, but prevention is a better plan. In the US, regular blood tests for the presence of infection are advised, coupled with appropriate preventative measures, so I would advise liaison with your veterinary surgeon.

For dogs travelling to heartworm-endemic areas of the EU, such as the Mediterranean coast, preventative treatment should be started before leaving the UK and maintained during the visit. Again, this is best arranged with your veterinary surgeon.

Heartworm is not currently a problem in the UK, but this is a situation that could change.

It is advisable to check your dogs for ticks if you have been for a ramble in the countryside.

EXTERNAL PARASITES

Fleas: There are several species of flea, which are not host-specific: not only can a dog be carrying cat and human fleas as well as dog fleas, but also the same flea treatment will kill and/or control them all. It is also accepted that environmental control is a vital part of a flea control programme. This is because the adult flea is only on the animal for as long as it takes to have a blood meal and to breed; the remainder of the lifecycle occurs in the house, car, caravan, shed...

There is a vast array of flea control products available, with various routes of administration: collar, powder, spray, 'spot-on', and oral. Flea control needs to be applied to all pets in the house (and that is independent of whether they leave the house since fleas can be introduced into the house by other pets and their human owners), so it is best to discuss your specific flea control needs with your vet.

Ticks: There were said to be classic pockets of ticks in the UK, such as in the New Forest and Thetford Forest, but they are actually found nationwide. The lifecycle is curious: each life stage takes a year to develop and move on to the next. Long grass is a major habitat. The vibration of animals moving through the grass stimulates the larva, nymph or adult to climb up a blade of grass and wave its legs in the air as it 'quests' for a host on to which to latch for its next blood meal. Humans are as likely to be hosts, so ramblers and orienteers are advised to cover their legs when going through rough, long grass, tucking the ends of their trousers into their socks.

As well as their presence causing irritation, it is the potential for disease that is of concern. A tick will transmit any infection previously contracted while feeding on an animal: for example Borrelia burgdorferi, the causal agent of Lyme disease (see page 134).

A-Z OF COMMON AILMENTS

ANAL SACS, IMPACTED

The anal sacs lie on either side of the back passage or anus at approximately four- and eight-o'-clock, if compared with the face of a clock. They fill with a particularly pungent fluid, which is emptied on to the faeces as they move past the sacs to exit from the anus. Theories abound as to why these sacs should become impacted periodically and seemingly more so in some dogs than others. The irritation of impacted anal sacs is often seen as 'scooting', when the backside is dragged along the ground. Some dogs will gnaw at their back feet or over the rump.

Increasing the fibre content of the diet helps some dogs; in others, there is underlying skin disease. It may be a one-off occurrence for no apparent reason. Sometimes, an infection can become established, requiring antibiotic therapy, which may need to be coupled with flushing out the infected sac under sedation or general anaesthesia. More rarely, a dog will present with an apparently acute-onset anal sac abscess, which is incredibly painful.

CALLUSES

Common in bigger dogs, such as the Labrador, a callus is a patch of thickened, hairless skin usually on the outside of the elbows but also occurring on the hocks, as a result of the pressure from lying on hard floors. Encouraging your dog to lie on soft bedding will help. Although generally a cosmetic problem, calluses can become infected.

CUTANEOUS HISTIOCYTOMA

This is usually on the paws or ear flaps of young dogs but can be anywhere else on the body as well, and sometimes on middle-aged individuals. My Labrador had one on a digit of a back paw when she was six years old. They may be first noticed when a few millimetres wide as a strawberry-like growth, which may grow to 10 or 15 millimetres wide (0.4-0.6 in). After two or three weeks, they usually simply vanish, although in the interim they may

have caused local itchiness. Occasionally, they may need to be surgically removed if proving very troublesome to the individual dog.

DIARRHOEA

Cause and treatment much as Gastritis (see below).

EAR INFECTIONS

The dog has a long external ear canal, initially vertical then horizontal, leading to the eardrum, which protects the middle ear. If your Labrador is shaking his head, then his ears will need to be inspected with an auroscope by a veterinary surgeon in order to identify any cause, and to ensure the eardrum is intact. A sample may be taken from the canal to be examined under the microscope and cultured to identify causal agents

before prescribing appropriate ear drops containing antibiotic, antifungal agent and/or steroid. Predisposing causes of otitis externa or infection in the external ear canal include:

- Presence of a foreign body, such as a grass awn.
- Ear mites, which are intensely irritating and stimulate the production of brown wax, predisposing to infection.
- Previous infections, causing the canal's lining to thicken, narrowing the canal and reducing ventilation.
- Swimming – most Labs simply adore swimming, but water trapped in the external ear canal can lead to infection, especially if the water is not clean!

FOREIGN BODIES

These can be internal or external. **Internal:** Items swallowed in haste without checking whether they will be digested can cause problems if they lodge in the stomach or obstruct the intestines, necessitating surgical removal. Acute vomiting is the main indication. Common objects I have seen removed include stones from the garden, peach stones, babies' dummies, golf balls, and once a lady's bra… It is possible to diagnose a dog with an intestinal obstruction across a waiting room from a particularly 'tucked-up' stance and pained facial expression. These patients bounce back from surgery dramatically. A previously docile and compliant obstructed patient will return for a post-operative check-up and literally bounce into the consulting room.

The Labrador is a hardy, outdoor dog, but he also enjoys his creature comforts.

External: Grass awns are adept at finding their way into orifices such as a nostril, down an ear, and into the soft skin between two digits (toes), whence they start a one-way journey due to the direction of their whiskers. In particular, I remember a grass awn that migrated from a hindpaw, causing abscesses along the way but not yielding itself up until it erupted through the skin in the groin!

GASTRITIS

This is usually a simple stomach upset, most commonly in response to dietary indiscretion. In the case of a Labrador, garbage gastritis is an even better description, because this breed is always on the look out for edible matter, during a walk or opportunistically within the home environment, such as the kitchen waste bin or the dustbin!

Scavenging constitutes a change in the diet as much as an abrupt switch in the food being fed by the owner. Generally, a day without food followed by a few days of small, frequent meals of a bland diet, such as cooked chicken or fish, or an appropriate prescription diet should allow the stomach to settle. It is vital to wean the patient back on to routine food or else another bout of gastritis may occur.

HYPOTHYROIDISM

This is the name given to an under-active thyroid gland. This is one of the more common hormonal disorders in the dog, manifesting in the young adult as weight gain that does not respond to normal dietary

Grass awns are a hazard in the summer, as they can enter the body and result in abscesses.

manipulation. There may be lethargy, and skin changes such as dandruff and non-specific itchiness as well. Once diagnosed with blood tests, supplementing with thyroid hormone should reverse the changes.

IDIOPATHIC TRIGEMINAL NEUROPATHY

Classically, a willing Labrador would carry his owner's wicker shopping basket and then be unable to close his mouth fully, but the cause is often not apparent. We were suddenly aware that our Labrador could not eat a biscuit and was drooling saliva excessively. She sat miserably in her basket over Christmas with her jaws partly open, unable to eat properly. Fortunately, this condition resolves of its own accord over the course of two or three weeks.

JOINT PROBLEMS

It is not unusual for older Labradors to be stiff after exercise, particularly in cold weather and especially if coupled with a swim, which most Labradors simply love. (See also Inherited disorders):

LUMPS

Regularly handling and stroking your dog will enable the early detection of lumps and bumps. These may be due to infection (abscess), bruising, multiplication of particular cells from within the body, or even an external parasite (tick). If you are worried about any lump you find, have it checked by a veterinary surgeon.

The Labrador seems to be predisposed to developing fatty lumps (lipomata). Sometimes, their sheer size, coupled with the position on the body, may cause problems, or if they grow and spread into surrounding tissues.

Mammary tumours are also common and should be checked by a veterinary surgeon as soon as they are found.

MOULTING

Having been brought up with Border Collies, who used to moult copious amounts of long fur, I had thought the Labrador would be easy to manage. In fact, with the fur being short, it is also very fine and seems to collect wherever it finds a corner or edge of the room. We seek to maintain a constant non-seasonal environment within our homes, which confuses the Labrador into seemingly moulting all year round! Regular grooming should help to keep things in check.

OVERWEIGHT

Being overweight does predispose to many other problems, such as diabetes mellitus, heart disease and joint problems. It is so easily prevented by simply acting as your Labrador's conscience. Ignore those eyes and feed according to your dog's waistline. The body condition is what matters qualitatively, alongside monitoring that individual's bodyweight as a quantitative measure. The Labrador should, in my opinion as a health professional, have at least a suggestion of a waist and it should be possible to feel the ribs beneath only a slight layer of fat.

Neutering does not automatically mean that your Labrador will be overweight. Having an ovario-hysterectomy does slow down the body's rate of working, castration to a lesser extent, but it therefore means that your dog needs less food, a lower energy intake. I recommend cutting back a little on the amount of food fed a few weeks before neutering to accustom your Labrador to less food. If she looks a little underweight on the morning of the operation, it will help the veterinary surgeon as well as giving her a little leeway weight-wise afterwards. It is always harder to lose weight after neutering than before, because of this slowing in the body's inherent metabolic rate.

ROLLING

When a Labrador rolls in fox muck, there is the potential for picking up a particular mite, resulting in sarcoptic mange. Fortunately, there are now specific licensed treatments.

SWIMMER'S OR LABRADOR TAIL

There are various other names for this, which manifests as a limpness of the tail such that it simply hangs down, apparently lifeless and immobile. It is so out-of-character for a Labrador not to wag his tail. It may develop the day after swimming when the tail

A Labrador will always tell you that he's hungry, but you must learn to resist his pleas.

The Labrador is a breed without exaggeration and therefore suffers few inherited disorders.

has been over-exercised in the water, or after excessive wagging, for example. Exposure to cold water, or even water that is too warm, can trigger it. Generally, it resolves within a few days. I prescribe a non-steroidal anti-inflammatory drug because it must be painful, or at least uncomfortable, unless contra-indicated by other health concerns.

TEETH PROBLEMS

Eating food starts with the canine teeth gripping and killing prey in the wild, incisor teeth biting off pieces of food, and the molar teeth chewing it. To be able to eat is vital for life, yet the actual health of the teeth is often overlooked: unhealthy teeth can predispose to disease, and not just by reducing the ability to eat. The presence of infection within the mouth can lead to bacteria entering the bloodstream and then filtering out at major organs, with the potential for serious consequences. That is not to forget that simply having dental pain can affect a dog's well-being,

as anyone who has had toothache will confirm.

The Labrador has a soft mouth for retrieving game, but will also carry other things, such as logs, resulting in worn and broken teeth. Eating stones, a habit some dogs have, will also damage the teeth.

Veterinary dentistry has made huge leaps in recent years, so that it no longer consists of extraction as the treatment of necessity.

Good dental health lies in the hands of the owner, starting from the moment the dog comes into your care. Just as we have taken on responsibility for feeding, so we have acquired the task of maintaining good dental and oral hygiene. In an ideal world, we should brush our dogs' teeth as regularly as our own. The Labrador puppy who finds having his teeth brushed is a huge game and excuse to roll over and over on the ground requires loads of patience, twice a day.

There are alternative strategies, ranging from dental chew-sticks to specially formulated foods, but the main thing is to be aware of

your dog's mouth. At least train your puppy to permit having his teeth examined, which will not only ensure you are checking in his mouth regularly but will also make your veterinary surgeon's job easier when there is a real need for your dog to 'Open wide!'

UVEAL CYST

You may notice one or more small, dark brown circular objects floating in the front of one or both of your Labrador's eyes, which do not seem to cause any problems.

INHERITED DISORDERS

Any individual, dog or human, may have an inherited disorder by virtue of genes acquired from the parents. This is significant not only for the health of that individual but also because of the potential for transmitting the disorder on to that individual's offspring and to subsequent generations, depending on the mode of inheritance.

There are control schemes in place for some inherited disorders. In the US, for example, the Canine Eye Registration

This is usually mild. It is a rolling outwards of the eyelids, which usually resolves as the dog grows and matures. It may predispose to conjunctivitis but is usually cosmetic and rarely requires corrective surgery (CERF).

ENTROPION

This is an inrolling of the eyelids. There are degrees of entropion, ranging from a slight inrolling to the more serious case requiring surgical correction because of the pain and damage to the surface of the eyeball (CERF).

EPILEPSY

Inheritance is suspected. This is often called juvenile epilepsy because it manifests in the immature and young adult Labrador (six months to three years old), with convulsions occurring singly or in clusters.

It is very alarming as an owner to see your dog having a fit, as you feel utterly helpless. It is vital to note when a fit or cluster of fits occurs on a calendar or in a diary, together with information about concurrent happenings (for example, family gathering, television switched on, fireworks, middle of the night).

Even if a young adult Labrador came to see me having had just one fit, I would be unlikely to start medication at once because 'every dog is allowed one or two fits'. Once medication has started, then one may never know whether or not he would have had any more fits at all. If it is needed to control the fits then medication will, from the nature of the problem, be life-long.

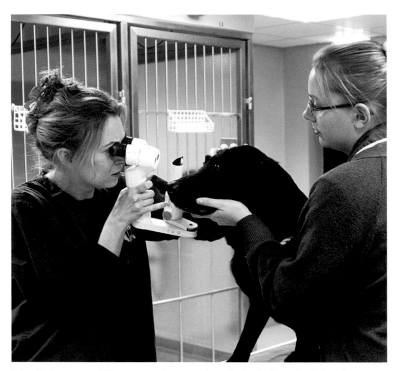

Inherited eye conditions occur in many breeds, including the Labrador.

Foundation (CERF) was set up by dog breeders concerned about heritable eye disease, and provides a database of dogs who have been examined by diplomates of the American College of Veterinary Ophthalmologists.

The major inherited disorders of concern in the Labrador Retriever are, in alphabetical order (not in any form of ranking):

ELBOW DYSPLASIA

This may first become apparent as a subtle forelimb lameness in the young juvenile Labrador who may also tend to sit with the affected leg slightly displaced, in order to bear less weight on the affected elbow. Flexion of the affected elbow during examination may be painful and resented! Older dogs with elbow dysplasia will be much stiffer than would be otherwise expected.

Elbow dysplasia is a progressive degenerative joint disease (arthritis) in response to one or more inherited features: ununited anconeal process, fragmented medial coronoid process, or osteochondritis of the medial humeral condyle. To be scored under the BVA/KC* and OFA*** Schemes, each elbow is radiographed at a position of extreme flexion and assessed on a scale of zero (unaffected) to three (severely affected).

HAEMOPHILIA

There are two forms, both of which are sex-linked recessive traits. In classic haemophilia or haemophilia A, there is a deficiency of blood-clotting factor VIII, whilst in haemophilia B it is factor IX that is affected. Both forms are carried on the X chromosome, meaning that bitches can be carriers while a male carrying one of the genes will be affected. Fortunately, haemophilia is extremely rare.

HEREDITARY CATARACT

There is a dominant pattern of inheritance. A cataract is a cloudiness of the lens of the eye. In the Labrador, this is the developmental form of hereditary cataract, occurring in the young or middle-aged dog, rather than the congenital form seen in other breeds (where some form of lens opacity is present from birth). Due to the position of the lens changes in affected Labradors, blindness is rare, fortunately. It is controlled under Schedule A of the BVA/KC/ISDS Scheme** in the UK, CERF in the US.

HIP DYSPLASIA

This is a malformation of the hip joints, causing pain, lameness and reduced exercise tolerance in the young Labrador, and resulting in degenerative joint disease (arthritis) in the older dog. Each hip joint is scored on several features to give a total of zero to 53 from a radiograph taken with the hips and pelvis in a specified position, usually requiring the dog to be sedated, after the age of one year under the BVA/KC Scheme*, from two

While your Labrador is growing, exercise should be limited, as putting too much stress on the joints can exacerbate conditions such as elbow dysplasia and hip dysplasia.

years of age in the US (OFA***).

LABRADOR RETRIEVER MYOPATHY

Also known as Floppy Labrador. This has an autosomal recessive mode of inheritance, and results in generalised muscle weakness. It manifests primarily as poor exercise tolerance from a very young age. There can also be difficulty in swallowing food because the muscles of the oesophagus (gullet) are also affected, causing it to balloon (megaoesophagus); this results in regurgitation of food, with the risk of food inhalation leading to pneumonia.

Life-span is reduced in most cases, depending on the severity of the condition. Mildly-affected Labradors can lead fairly normal lives with the help of simple strategies. For example, feeding from a height will help reduce regurgitation by harnessing the pull of gravity.

TRICUSPID VALVE DYSPLASIA (TVD)

There seems to be an increasing occurrence of TVD in the Labrador. This is a congenital heart defect: an affected individual is born with a malformed heart valve between the two chambers of the right side of the heart. The

Some Labradors may benefit from complementary therapies, but this route should be pursued under veterinary supervision.

heart's ability to act as a pump depends on the integrity of its valves. A wide spectrum of effect is seen, ranging from a slight malformation having little effect on life-span, across to such a leaky valve that congestive heart failure develops while young.

Blood leaking back through the valve causes turbulence in the blood flow, and the normally clear click as the valve closes is muffled. This is heard as a murmur when a stethoscope is placed on the chest wall, especially over the valve, so that a common time to first suspect TVD is when a veterinary surgeon examines the puppy as a first health check or prior to starting a vaccination course. A detailed ultrasound examination is needed to diagnose and stage the extent of the problem.

RETINAL DEFECTS
Central progressive retinal atrophy, generalised progressive retinal atrophy, multifocal retinal dysplasia, and total retinal dysplasia are each controlled under Schedule A of the **BVA/KC/ISDS Scheme in the UK, CERF in the US.

* British Veterinary Association/Kennel Club Scheme
** British Veterinary Association/Kennel Club/International Sheepdog Society Scheme
*** Orthopedic Foundation for Animals, US

COMPLEMENTARY THERAPIES
Just as for human health, I do believe there is a place for alternative therapies but alongside

and complementing orthodox treatment under the supervision of a veterinary surgeon. That is why 'complementary therapies' is a better name.

Because animals do not have a choice, there are measures in place to safeguard their well-being and welfare. All manipulative treatment must be under the direction of a veterinary surgeon who has examined the patient and diagnosed the condition that she or he feels needs that form of treatment. This covers physiotherapy, chiropractic, osteopathy and swimming therapy. For example, dogs with arthritis who cannot exercise as freely as they were accustomed will enjoy the sensation of controlled non-weight-bearing exercise in water, and benefit with improved muscling and overall fitness.

All other complementary therapies, such as acupuncture, homoeopathy and aromatherapy, can only be carried out by veterinary surgeons who have been trained in that particular field. Acupuncture is mainly used in dogs for pain relief, often to good effect. The needles look more alarming to the owner, but they are very fine and are well tolerated by most canine patients. Speaking personally, superficial needling is not unpleasant and does help with pain relief.

Homoeopathy has had a mixed press in recent years. It is based on the concept of treating like with like. Additionally, a homeopathic remedy is said to become more powerful the more it is diluted.

The Labrador is great fun to live with, as well as being a loyal and loving companion. Make sure you keep your half of the bargain and give him all the care he needs.

SUMMARY

As the owner of a Labrador, you are responsible for his care and health. Not only must you make decisions on his behalf, you are also responsible for establishing a lifestyle for him that will ensure he leads a long and happy life.

Diet plays as important a part in this as exercise, for example. Nutritional manipulation has a long history. Formulation of animal feedstuffs is aimed at optimising production from, for example, dairy cattle. For the domestic dog, it is only in recent years that the need has been recognised for changing the diet to suit the dog as he grows, matures and then enters his twilight years. So called life-stage diets try to match the nutritional needs of the dog as he progresses through life.

A working dog food will suit the Labrador working as a gundog, but it may be prudent to return to a more standard food in the quiet season, for the sake of your dog's waistline! There are also foods for those Labradors tactfully termed as obese-prone, such as those who have been neutered or are less active than others, or simply like their food. Do remember, though, that ultimately you are in control of your Labrador's diet, unless he is able to profit from scavenging!

On the other hand, prescription diets are of necessity fed under the supervision of a veterinary surgeon because each is formulated to meet the very specific needs of particular health conditions. Should a prescription diet be fed to a healthy dog, or to a dog with a different illness, there could be adverse effects.

It is important to remember that your Labrador has no choice. As his owner, you are responsible for any decision made, so it must be as informed a decision as possible. Always speak to your veterinary surgeon if you have any worries about your Labrador. He is not just a dog, because he will have become a definite member of the family from the moment you brought him home.

THE CONTRIBUTORS

EDITOR: DAVID CRAIG (DAVRICARD)

David cannot remember a time when his family did not have a dog – usually Yorkshire Terriers when he was a child – and when he was 12 his parents bought him his first Labrador. David's first show ring success came with Sh. Ch. Bradking Bridgette of Davricard, bred by Arthur and Peggy Kelley of the famous Bradking kennels. David was only 17 years old when she became a Champion. His first home-bred Champion was Sh. Ch. Davricard Bobby Shafto, who gained his title and sired Champions and CC winners here and abroad before leaving for the States.

The first time David saw Bradking Hugo was when he was a promising eight-week-old puppy. He went on to campaign Hugo to his title at 14 months of age, to being top Labrador in the UK for three years, and in breaking the CC breed record before retiring gracefully at the age of five years after winning his 50th CC. In partnership with Angela Williams, David has made up four more Labrador Champions.

David began judging when he was 17 years old and has awarded CCs in the UK to Labradors since 1992. He has judged in most European countries, the United States and Australia, and is greatly looking forward to judging Labrador dogs at Crufts in 2010. See *Chapter Seven: The Perfect Labrador.*

LYNDA HERON (BRIGBURN)

Lynda has owned and bred Labrador Retrievers for over 27 years. She has made up three full Champions who have all been regulars on local shoots, and she has also bred a Field Trial award winner. Lynda has judged Labradors all over the world, including Canada, USA, Russia, Japan, and many countries in Europe. She is a former Chairman of the Northumberland and Durham Labrador Club and is currently an active member of the Breed Council's Health sub-committee. See *Chapter One: Getting to Know Labrador Retrievers.*

ANNE TAYLOR (FABRACKEN)

As a child Anne's main interest was horses – then her first Labrador arrived. She caught the showing bug, and in time Candy produced a bitch who went on to be her first major winner.

Anne later bought a bitch from the famous Poolstead kennel, who gained her Show Champion title and introduced Anne to the working Labrador world because her ambition was to make her bitch into a full Champion.

Now 41 years on from her original Labrador, and with a number of Champions at home and abroad, Anne's enthusiasm for the breed, and especially for seeing it work as a gundog, is as great as ever. She has travelled all over the world, judging Labradors. See *Chapter Two: The First Labradors.*

MARGARET BROWN (RAMSAYVILLE)

Margaret, and her husband, Andrew, have owned Labradors since 1973 and have enjoyed considerable success showing their dogs under the Ramsayville affix. Their daughter, Mairi, shares a love for dogs, and they now work as a team, with Margaret handling the dogs in the ring.

Although the family do not claim to be 'big breeders', to date their dogs have won over 100 Challenge Certificates and Reserve Challenge Certificates. Margaret's first 'show' Labrador was from the Poolstead kennel owned by Bob and Didi Hepworth, and she proved to be a fine brood bitch. She was quickly followed by three Balrion King Frost daughters, two yellow Labs and a black Lab from the Sudeo kennel, owned by Maurice Givan. These four bitches were the foundation of Ramsayville, but, more importantly, they were lovely Labradors to own, each with their individual personality.

Margaret's passion for dogs has given her the opportunity to judge all over the world. She remains indebted to her beloved Labradors for making it all possible. See *Chapter Three: A Labrador For Your Lifestyle.*

ANN M. BRITTON (BOWSTONES)

Ann was born into a well-known dog-showing family; the fourth generation descended from Victorian forebears whose lady pioneers re-launched the Ladies Kennel Association in 1904. The Bowstones prefix was registered with the Kennel Club in 1946 by her mother, a Toy and Utility judge, who also bred gundogs and Champion Cavalier King Charles and Shih Tzus. Ann attended her first dog show, Crufts, in 1948 and has been involved with showing and breeding dogs, and organising Championship dog shows most of her life.

Ann, an international Labrador judge, breeds and shows Labradors and owns four homebred Champions plus other top winners. She has been the weekly Labrador columnist for *Our Dogs* magazine for the past nine years, reviews books and writes articles for Labrador periodicals and general dog magazines both at home and abroad. See *Chapter Four: The New Arrival.*

JOY VENTURI-ROSE (LEOSPRING)

Joy has owned a small kennel of black and yellow Labradors (with a particular interest in the fox red colour) for 25 years under the Leospring affix. Temperament is the first consideration, and she has always been interested in breeding and training good-looking dogs who can work well. Close attention is paid to using the KC/BVA health schemes. With her husband, Chris,, most of their dogs have won both at field trials as well as in the Championship Show ring. Joy is on the KC Field Trial judges B panel, is a Championship show judge and has judged in nine different countries. She is Field Trial Secretary of the Kent Surrey and Sussex Labrador Club, Chairman of the Hampshire Gundog Society, and sits on the Committee of the Labrador Retriever Club where she organises the annual Gundog Water Test and the Show Gundog Qualifying Trial. She is also a member of the KC Labrador Breed Council Health Committee and is a breed note writer for the *Dog World* newspaper. See *Chapter Five: The Best of Care.*

JULIA BARNES

Julia has owned and trained Labrador Retrievers for many years, and is a puppy socialiser for Dogs for the Disabled. A former journalist, she has written many books, including several on dog training and behaviour.
See *Chapter Six: Training and Socialisation.*

ALISON LOGAN MA VetMB MRCVS

Alison qualified as a veterinary surgeon from Cambridge University in 1989, having been brought up surrounded by all manner of animals and birds in the north Essex countryside. She has been in practice in her home town ever since, living with her husband, two children and Labrador Retriever Pippin.

She contributes on a regular basis to *Veterinary Times, Veterinary Nurse Times, Dogs Today, Cat World* and *Pet Patter,* the PetPlan newsletter. In 1995, Alison won the Univet Literary Award with an article on Cushing's disease, and she won it again (as the Vetoquinol Literary Award) in 2002, writing about common conditions in the Shar-Pei.
See *Chapter Eight: Happy and Healthy.*

USEFUL ADDRESSES

KENNEL & BREED CLUBS

UK
The Kennel Club
1 Clarges Street, London, W1J 8AB
Tel: 0870 606 6750
Fax: 0207 518 1058
Web: www.the-kennel-club.org.uk

To obtain up-to-date contact information for the following breed clubs, please contact the Kennel Club:
- Cotswold and Wyevern Labrador Club
- East Anglian Labrador Club
- Kent, Surrey and Sussex Labrador Retriever Club
- Labrador Club of Scotland
- Labrador Retriever Club
- Labrador Retriever Club of Northern Ireland
- Labrador Retriever Club of Wales
- Midland Counties Labrador Retriever Club
- North West Labrador Retriever Club
- Northumberland and Durham Labrador Retriever Club
- Three Ridings Labrador Club
- West of England Labrador Retriever Club
- Yellow Labrador Club

USA
American Kennel Club (AKC)
5580 Centerview Drive,
Raleigh, NC 27606, USA.
Tel: 919 233 9767
Fax: 919 233 3627
Email: info@akc.org
Web: www.akc.org

United Kennel Club (UKC)
100 E Kilgore Rd, Kalamazoo,
MI 49002-5584, USA.
Tel: 269 343 9020
Fax: 269 343 7037
Web: www.ukcdogs.com/

Labrador Retriever Club of America, Inc.
Web: http://www.thelabradorclub.com

For contact details of regional clubs, please contact the Labrador Retriever Club of America.

AUSTRALIA
Australian National Kennel Council (ANKC)
The Australian National Kennel Council is the administrative body for pure breed canine affairs in Australia. It does not, however, deal directly with dog exhibitors, breeders or judges. For information pertaining to breeders, clubs or shows, please contact the relevant State or Territory Controlling Body.

Dogs Australian Capital Territory
PO Box 815, Dickson ACT 2602
Tel: (02) 6241 4404
Fax: (02) 6241 1129
Email: administrator@dogsact.org.au
Web: www.dogsact.org.au

Dogs New South Wales
PO Box 632, St Marys, NSW 1790
Tel: (02) 9834 3022 or 1300 728 022 (NSW Only)
Fax: (02) 9834 3872
Email: info@dogsnsw.org.au
Web: www.dogsnsw.org.au

Dogs Northern Territory
PO Box 37521, Winnellie NT 0821
Tel: (08) 8984 3570
Fax: (08) 8984 3409
Email: admin@dogsnt.com.au
Web: www.dogsnt.com.au

Dogs Queensland
PO Box 495, Fortitude Valley Qld 4006
Tel: (07) 3252 2661
Fax: (07) 3252 3864
Email: info@dogsqueensland.org.au
Web: www.dogsqueensland.org.au

Dogs South Australia
PO Box 844
Prospect East SA 5082
Tel: (08) 8349 4797
Fax: (08) 8262 5751
Email: info@dogssa.com.au
Web: www.dogssa.com.au

Tasmanian Canine Association Inc
The Rothman Building
PO Box 116
Glenorchy Tas 7010
Tel: (03) 6272 9443
Fax: (03) 6273 0844
Email: tca@iprimus.com.au
Web: www.tasdogs.com

Dogs Victoria
Locked Bag K9
Cranbourne VIC 3977
Tel: (03)9788 2500
Fax: (03) 9788 2599
Email: office@dogsvictoria.org.au
Web: www.dogsvictoria.org.au

Dogs Western Australia
PO Box 1404
Canning Vale WA 6970
Tel: (08) 9455 1188
Fax: (08) 9455 1190
Email: k9@dogswest.com
Web: www.dogswest.com

INTERNATIONAL
Fédération Cynologique Internationalé (FCI)/World Canine Organisation
Place Albert 1er, 13, B-6530 Thuin,
Belgium.
Tel: +32 71 59.12.38
Fax: +32 71 59.22.29
Web: www.fci.be/

TRAINING AND BEHAVIOUR

UK
Association of Pet Dog Trainers
PO Box 17, Kempsford, GL7 4WZ
Telephone: 01285 810811
Email: APDToffice@aol.com
Web: http://www.apdt.co.uk

Association of Pet Behaviour Counsellors
PO BOX 46, Worcester, WR8 9YS
Telephone: 01386 751151
Fax: 01386 750743
Email: info@apbc.org.uk
Web: http://www.apbc.org.uk/

USA
Association of Pet Dog Trainers
101 North Main Street, Suite 610
Greenville, SC 29601, USA.
Tel: 1 800 738 3647
Email: information@apdt.com
Web: www.apdt.com/

American College of Veterinary Behaviorists
College of Veterinary Medicine, 4474 Tamu,
Texas A&M University
College Station, Texas 77843-4474
Web: http://dacvb.org/

American Veterinary Society of Animal Behavior
Web: www.avsabonline.org/

AUSTRALIA
APDT Australia Inc
PO Box 3122, Bankstown Square, NSW 2200.
Email: secretary@apdt.com.au
Web: www.apdt.com.au

Canine Behaviour
For details of regional behaviourists, contact the relevant State or Territory Controlling Body.

ACTIVITIES

UK
Agility Club
http://www.agilityclub.co.uk/

British Flyball Association
PO Box 990, Doncaster, DN1 9FY
Telephone: 01628 829623
Email: secretary@flyball.org.uk
Web: http://www.flyball.org.uk/

Field Trials
Kennel Club Field Trials
Secretary: Anne Greeves
Honeycomb, 29 Low Road, Grimston,
Kings Lynn, Norfolk. PE32 1AE.
Telephone: 01485 600918 or 07921 451273

Working Trials
36 Elwyndene Road, March, Cambridgeshire,
PE15 9RL.
www.workingtrials.co.uk

North American Dog Agility Council
P.O. Box 1206, Colbert,
OK 74733, USA.
Web: www.nadac.com/

North American Flyball Association, Inc.
1333 West Devon Avenue, #512
Chicago, IL 60660
Tel/Fax: 800 318 6312
Email: flyball@flyball.org
Web: www.flyball.org/

Field Trials
Contact the AKC or UKC.

AUSTRALIA

Agility Dog Association of Australia
ADAA Secretary, PO Box 2212,
Gailes, QLD 4300, Australia.
Tel: 0423 138 914
Email: admin@adaa.com.au
Web: www.adaa.com.au/

NADAC Australia (North American Dog Agility Council - Australian Division)
12 Wellman Street, Box Hill South, Victoria 3128, Australia.
Email: shirlene@nadacaustralia.com
Web: www.nadacaustralia.com/

Australian Flyball Association
PO Box 4179, Pitt Town, NSW 2756
Tel: 0407 337 939
Email: info@flyball.org.au
Web: www.flyball.org.au/

Field Trials
Contact relevant state authority.

INTERNATIONAL

World Canine Freestyle Organisation
P.O. Box 350122, Brooklyn, NY 11235-2525,
USA
Tel: (718) 332-8336
Fax: (718) 646-2686
Email: wcfodogs@aol.com
Web: www.worldcaninefreestyle.org

HEALTH

UK

Alternative Veterinary Medicine Centre
Chinham House, Stanford in the Vale,
Oxfordshire, SN7 8NQ
Tel: 01367 710324
Fax: 01367 718243
Web: www.alternativevet.org/

British Small Animal Veterinary Association
Woodrow House, 1 Telford Way,
Waterwells Business Park, Quedgeley,
Gloucestershire, GL2 2AB
Tel: 01452 726700
Fax: 01452 726701
Email: customerservices@bsava.com
Web: http://www.bsava.com/

Royal College of Veterinary Surgeons
Belgravia House, 62-64 Horseferry Road,
London, SW1P 2AF

Tel: 0207 222 2001
Fax: 0207 222 2004
Email: admin@rcvs.org.uk
Web: www.rcvs.org.uk

USA

American Holistic Veterinary Medical Association
2218 Old Emmorton Road
Bel Air, MD 21015
Tel: 410 569 0795
Fax 410 569 2346
Email: office@ahvma.org
Web: www.ahvma.org/

American Veterinary Medical Association
1931 North Meacham Road, Suite 100,
Schaumburg, IL 60173-4360, USA.
Tel: 800 248 2862
Fax: 847 925 1329
Web: www.avma.org

American College of Veterinary Surgeons
19785 Crystal Rock Dr, Suite 305
Germantown, MD 20874, USA.
Tel: 301 916 0200
Toll Free: 877 217 2287
Fax: 301 916 2287
Email: acvs@acvs.org
Web: www.acvs.org/

AUSTRALIA

Australian Holistic Vets
Web: www.ahv.com.au/

Australian Small Animal Veterinary Association
40/6 Herbert Street, St Leonards, NSW 2065,
Australia.
Tel: 02 9431 5090
Fax: 02 9437 9068
Email: asava@ava.com.au
Web: www.asava.com.au

Australian Veterinary Association
Unit 40, 6 Herbert Street, St Leonards, NSW
2065, Australia.
Tel: 02 9431 5000
Fax: 02 9437 9068
Web: www.ava.com.au

Australian College Veterinary Scientists
Building 3, Garden City Office Park,
2404 Logan Road, Eight Mile Plains,
Queensland 4113, Australia.
Tel: 07 3423 2016
Fax: 07 3423 2977
Email: admin@acvs.org.au
Web: http://acvsc.org.au

ASSISTANCE DOGS

Canine Partners
Mill Lane, Heyshott, Midhurst,
, GU29 0ED
Tel: 08456 580480
Fax: 08456 580481
Web: www.caninepartners.co.uk

Dogs for the Disabled
The Frances Hay Centre, Blacklocks Hill,
Banbury, Oxon, OX17 2BS

Tel: 01295 252600
Web: www.dogsforthedisabled.org

Guide Dogs for the Blind Association
Burghfield Common, Reading, RG7 3YG
Tel: 01189 835555
Fax: 01189 835433
Web: www.guidedogs.org.uk/

Hearing Dogs for Deaf People
The Grange, Wycombe Road, Saunderton,
Princes Risborough, Bucks, HP27 9NS
Tel: 01844 348100
Fax: 01844 348101
Web: www.hearingdogs.org.uk

Pets as Therapy
3a Grange Farm Cottages, Wycombe Road,
Saunderton, Princes Risborough,
Bucks, HP27 9NS
Tel: 01845 345445
Fax: 01845 550236
Web: http://www.petsastherapy.org/

Support Dogs
21 Jessops Riverside, Brightside Lane,
Sheffield, S9 2RX
Tel: 01142 617800
Fax: 01142 617555
Email: supportdogs@btconnect.com
Web: www.support-dogs.org.uk

USA

Therapy Dogs International
88 Bartley Road, Flanders, NJ 07836,.
Tel: 973 252 9800
Fax: 973 252 7171
Email: tdi@gti.net
Web: www.tdi-dog.o

Therapy Dogs Inc.
P.O. Box 20227, Cheyenne, WY 82003.
Tel: 307 432 0272.
Fax: 307-638-2079
Web: www.therapydogs.com

Delta Society - Pet Partners
875 124th Ave NE, Suite 101 • Bellevue, WA
98005 USA.
Email: info@DeltaSociety.org
Web: www.deltasociety.org

Comfort Caring Canines
8135 Lare Street, Philadelphia, PA 19128.
Email: ccc@comfortcaringcanines.org
Web: www.comfortcaringcanines.org/

AUSTRALIA

AWARE Dogs Australia, Inc
PO Box 883, Kuranda, Queensland, 488,
Australia.
Tel: 07 4093 8152
Web: www.awaredogs.org.au/

Delta Society — Therapy Dogs
Web: www.deltasociety.com.au